LIMA BEANS
AND
CITY CHICKEN

MARTINA DURBIN

LIMA BEANS AND CITY CHICKEN

A Memoir of the Open Hearth

E. P. DUTTON   NEW YORK

Published in the United States of America by E. P. Dutton,
a division of NAL Penguin Inc.,
2 Park Avenue, New York, N.Y. 10016.

Published simultaneously in Canada
by Fitzhenry and Whiteside, Limited, Toronto.

Library of Congress Cataloging-in-Publication Data
Durbin, Martina.
Lima beans and city chicken: a memoir of the open hearth
Martina Durbin.—1st ed.
p.   cm.
ISBN 0-525-24722-X
1. Durbin, Martina—Family.   2. Reisz family.   3. Dombrowski
family.   4. Polish Americans—Biography.   5. United States—
Biography.   6. Labor and laboring classes—United States—
Biography.   I. Title.
CT275.D8845A3   1988
929'.2'089918507—dc19
88-18986
CIP
Designed by REM Studio

1 3 5 7 9 10 8 6 4 2

First Edition

Is a writer allowed to dedicate a book more than once? I mean, is it OK to dedicate a book to more than one person—the same book? I surely hope so, because I'm going to do just that. . . .

To Larry Kramer, poet/teacher/friend, who once told me I was a "real poet," and who just kept saying, "Of course you can. . . ." He backed his faith in me with hours of work, and reading, and gallons of hot coffee, and with the gift of a beautiful whippet named Clementine.

To my family—Big Dave, Lovely Vanessa, and Wonderful Christopher, who say they love me and make me believe it. Also to Lizbeth, for the gift of an authentic and loving place to be whatever it is I am.

To Stephen Dunn for his validation, his time, his goodness to me.

To Kathleen Clarke Bayard and Patrick Joseph O'Reilly for being the kind of friends who kick your ass when it's necessary, then give you an ice pack for the pain.

To Michael Wilds and Theodore Humphrey and David Fite and Victor Okada and the whole damn English department at Cal Poly Pomona—you all know what for.

To Yaddo, thank you for having me.

Now, *that's* what I call a dedication. . . .

Contents

*Everything you're about to read is true
except for the facts
and one or two other things.
Right, Dad?*

Introduction

If you were invited to my parents' house during the holidays, or for a birthday party, or a barbecue or any other kind of celebration, everyone there would sit around and tell stories—stories about wonderful kinds of trouble they were all in at one time or another, silliness and adventures and the things of life that are important to tell about, because those are the things necessary to know. For instance, one of my aunts was once in *Who's Who in America*. She was a very smart, important woman who did a lot of innovative things in the field of social work in the state of Ohio. Pretty impressive, right? You know what's *really* important about her? My aunt weighed about 285 pounds. She was about 5'3" tall and had a temper that would put a bull elephant to shame. She could make her two brothers (my father and his brother Louie) shut up with a twitch of her eyebrow; she could make them behave with a hard look; she could pick them up and throw them across the room for their various misbehaviors, and often did that, even if she merely suspected misbehaving. She collected diamonds. I'm not kidding. She collected uncut, unmounted diamonds, which she carried around in a black velvet bag in her purse. She showed them to me once when I was having lunch with her at a great little inn at Oberlin College. She dumped them out on the table in front of me like they were jacks and said, "Damn prettiest things there are in the world."

These are true things about her; they have nothing to do with *Who's Who in America,* and they're a whole lot more interesting. There are many such people in this book.

Allow me to introduce you to them. First, meet my father, John Reisz, and my mother, Mary Reisz, who is often called "Marcia." My father's brother is Lou—Uncle

Louie—his spitfire wife is Margie. My father's sister is Marie, and her husband is Gib—my Uncle Gibby. My mother's sister is Jan and her husband is Phil. My grandpa was named John, but you'll only read about him as "Grandpa."

You are going to have the pleasure of getting to know Andy Kushner, Bob Butler, Little Billy Marshall, and a few of the women in their lives. They were my father's dearest, truest friends. He called them his "chums." You'll get acquainted with some of my mother's friends and you'll meet my old buddy, Paulette-from-up-the-street. (I have no idea of what happened to her, but hardly a week goes by that I don't think of her.)

You'll also meet my Great-Uncle Tony and my Uncle Joe from my mother's side of the family; they're both good guys, as is my Uncle Jay, who is married to mother's sister Helen.

There might be a couple of other assorted friends and relatives here and there, but I think I've mentioned the main members of my Cast of Characters. Such good people—all of them—probably a lot like the people in your own family. So, read on. I think you'll have fun with these folks.

Remember something while you're reading, if you will: The things you will read in this book come from the memories, and then from the mouths, of many people. Things that are told and retold in the family with different nuances and variations, depending on who's telling them. So sometimes the name of a store or the name of a cousin who said something-or-other might not be *exactly* the way it *exactly* happened, but it's the way it was told to me, so it's the way I will tell it to you.

What you're about to read aren't just happy little memories or a bit of pleasant history. They're more than that. You're going to be reading about a time when there was something more to living than finding and reaching one's career goals, or being into "upward mobility," or having anxiety attacks over whether or not a "hard body" can be attained in six months. This book is about a time when there were *possibilities*.

In 1949, we lived near Fontana, California, where my father worked for Kaiser Steel Corporation. He was a millwright, and we were the family of a millwright, which was a very fine thing to be. The baggage of being a millwright's family was this: a most marvelous and unusual collection of friends and friends of friends and parties and barbecues and evenings at a bar called Domenic's and wild times with the union—strikes and negotiations and picket lines and shop stewards—and, of course, stories.

There were, as I mentioned, *possibilities,* and, too, there were dreams. Steel town dreams are not much different from other kinds. Oh, a little smaller, maybe...a little more accessible...but dreams just the same. They are the dreams tied up in Saturday mornings with a lawnmower, doughnuts for breakfast, Easter next Sunday with Polish sausage, lamb cake, a raise in the next paycheck, a settlement negotiated with no strike necessary, Christmas in a month with stuffed cabbages and pork roast and poppyseed/prune/nut pastry to be dunked in coffee on Christmas morning, a plumbing problem that can maybe be fixed by a clever brother-in-law who owes you a favor, an only daughter's good grades, friends and their floozy ladies on a real warm Sunday in June, before the barbecued chicken and baking powder biscuits are ready to eat, payday evening at Domenic's bar when it's raining outside and everybody inside is still wearing blast furnace smiles. These are the kinds of things that people a millwright's dreams and all of them are wound around with an amazing amount of love and good cheer.

I guess I have to come clean with it: This book is just an excuse, really. It's just a way to tell you how much I loved it all. Fontana, Kaiser Steel, the Santa Ana winds, the conversation, the steel mill smell on my father's clothes—I loved it all. But I can't very well walk up to people on the street and say, "Hey! There was this Time and I want you to sit down while I tell you about it," or, "Why don't you and a couple hundred other folks come on over. We'll have Lima Beans and City Chicken and I'll tell you some stories that'll make you forget Wall Street, or your computer, or your agoraphobic wife, or your bulimic daughter, or your difficulties with the gardener." I can't do that, can I? So, I wrote this book about all of it.

Of course, my father would say that I *should* invite you all. He'd say, "Forgodsakes, Honey. Ask them over. Mom can add some more beans to the pot and we'll ask some of the guys to bring over an extra six-pack or two." My father has always loved an audience—nearly as much as he loves Lima Beans and City Chicken. He'd tell me to ask you anyway so he could be the one to tell the stories.

Well, anyway...that's why I wrote this book. I just wanted to tell somebody that there was this Time....

LIMA BEANS
AND
CITY CHICKEN

1

Something
About My Father

I'm not sure if it was the undershirts or what; I only know that there was a time when there was magic in men. You're hearing that from a feminist, a true pioneer in the movement, which ought to make it more valid. Anyway, there was this Time and I think it had something to do with the undershirts. You know the kind: white with straps that went over the shoulder and made every man look as if he had muscle-y arms and shoulders even if he was your wimpy cousin Mike who didn't have a real muscle in his whole body.

My father was born in Hungary. I think there was an Austrian Duke or a Prince or some kind of royalty in the family one hundred years ago (Hungarians always claim royalty), and they all got displaced or something, so my father's family ended up being working people. They came to America, and settled in a steel town in Ohio—not a town made of steel, you understand, but a town that produces steel. That's where Dad grew up. He worked, went to school, sold papers, played basketball, worked, dated, brawled, womanized and whored a bit, with the steel mill pumping grit every minute all over his red hair.

A book is supposed to have structure. I'd love to give you that, but it's going to be rough. I don't remember things in a very organized way. My recollections are like a good salsa recipe—I never make it the same way, but it always tastes the same. So, I'm going to ask you to bear with me if I don't structure this thing like the creative writing classes tell you to do it. I'm not putting up dry wall here, I'm remembering. It's very different.

My father was always a man who dearly loved the ladies. As a youngster, he got to know them selling papers on the street corner nearest the town whorehouse. Those ladies liked Dad as much as he liked them, so he always sold all his papers, got great tips, and received an education worthy of his ancestry. He played basketball for the YMCA, went to church on Sunday, and ran errands for his mother, who doted on him. When he finally quit selling papers and went into semi-pro basketball, there must have been some powerful crying and gnashing of teeth. He went to a lot of different places around Ohio, playing ball, then quit that and worked in the mills again, then went to work for the WPA during the Depression, then back to the mills because he couldn't join the service (punctured eardrums). I'm going through this part quickly because it is not the part I like best. I want to get to the part about the ladies and Dad. I'm talking about a good-looking man: dark red hair, wide social smile, bright brown eyes, and (they tell me) very fast hands—all that basketball practice, I guess. He was a pretty compassionate person, too. He knew that there were a lot of women and only one of him, so he was determined to spread himself around so that everyone got a little bit—even the not-so-pretty ones, even the already married ones, even the ones with big boyfriends.

Once upon a time, my father was very good friends with a man who owned a bar. The man had a pudgy, blond wife who stood on the customer side of the bar, talking with the customers and doing other important PR work essential to the success of the business. I swear to you, the woman's name was Millie. She fell in love with my father's red hair and began pursuing him with a passion once reserved for her husband and maybe just a very few others. My father resisted her as long as he could (thirty-four minutes, I think is what he said) but finally gave in to his baser instincts and laid the lovely lady... only a few times, he said. When the affair had become tiresome to Dad, he talked with the woman, explained his "rolling-stone-gathers-no-moss" philosophy, and went off with his brother to find another bar to frequent. That should have been the end of this story, but it wasn't. Millie had a little trouble with this decision of Dad's. She cried, she pulled her hair out (and some of his), she swore, she began following Dad everywhere and, although she threatened misery, mayhem, and suicide, he was unshakable in his resolve to leave her to her husband, Chet.

Now, once upon another time, my father and his handsome, small, short-tempered older brother, Lou, met two beautiful young women at a basketball game.

"Could you two ladies be persuaded to go to a movie with us?" invited my father.

"And, after the movie, how about a hot dog and a short snort, just to be friendly," said hopeful Uncle Lou.

The dear ladies were indeed persuaded. They giggled, lowered their eyes, and said yes, and even went along to sit in the park (in the car in the dark) at lakeside late that same night to watch the "submarine races." All these fine things came to pass, but, as the happy group began to leave the moonlit park, strange sounds emanated from the rear of the car.

My father, with the sense of foreboding often given to the promiscuous, opened the trunk and a somewhat sweaty lump of pudgy, blond lady fell out shouting, "I love you! I love you! Don't do this to me!"

"Millie," said my dad, "you can see I'm entertaining. Go home. You smell like a spare tire." And he shut the trunk, got in the car and drove away.

I like that story very much. It is now and always was hilarious to me. I heard it the first time from my Uncle

Lou (from others later), who told it while I sat on the floor between his legs, the top of my head getting wet from the dewy stuff dropping off his beer glass.

It's always been strange to me to hear people say that they couldn't picture their fathers or mothers being drunk or foolish or horsing around with anonymous others. I've never had any trouble visualizing those things. I can see clearly a picture of my 5′9″ father and his 5′4″ brother hollering. "OK, you sonsofbitches—come and get it!" at a barroom full of 6-foot 300-pound steel workers whose women were in danger of being set upon by Jack "Red" Reisz and his crazy brother Lou.

I've been told that everybody's earliest memories are of their parents. That's why I started with all this stuff about my father. It leads to all the other things that I remember, the best of which have to do with Dad and Domenic's. I'll get to that later on.

2

The Time
the Bed Caught Fire
and Another Story

My father has always been a firm believer in friendships. His circle of companions was a large one and was not confined, as I've already said, to one gender. He believed that a woman could be as good a friend to a guy as a man could, with some terrific side benefits. For instance, Dad said that he wouldn't mind working side by side with a woman in the Open Hearth because he bet she'd smell a damn sight better after the workday was over. I asked him once if he minded having just me for a kid because I was a girl and would he rather I'd been a boy? He said "No, Honey. Hell! Some of my best friends have been girls. You just stay a girl, Muggsy —you'll do fine." I thought that over a long time before I decided that he'd said a good thing. Anyway, he liked females even if they turned on him, which they almost always did as far as I could tell. I'm going to tell you a story that I heard at least one hundred times in at least fifty different versions. My mother didn't like this story much—none of the versions—but that fact never stopped anyone in our house from telling it. I guess I'll tell it to you the way my Uncle Lou told it because he liked to tell the stories so they'd make all the good guys look blameless (the "good guys" being him and my father).

Dad and Uncle Lou were once involved with a couple of twin sisters whose names were Winifred and Virginia. The story takes a very poetic turn here—see what's coming?—as the sisters were affectionately known as Winnie and Ginny. When I was ten years old, this story became hilarious to me as soon as I heard those names. The girls were very nearly identical, Dad said, except that Winnie's hair was a little darker than Ginny's. That's how you could tell them apart.

"Also," my uncle said, "Winnie could drink more than you or I put together, Jack."

"She could not. She'd drink her drink about halfway down and then dump the rest in my glass to impress everybody."

"She'd dump it in your glass, all right, and then drink it. I was sure impressed. That woman could still get on her feet and walk out of the bar when you and I were settled in for the night and wondering how the hell we were going to explain again to Ma why we didn't come home." (About this time, I'd ask, "How come you didn't go home, Dad?" And Dad would say, "Honey, we were so drunk, we'd never—" Then Mother would clear her throat and say, "Jack." And I knew I was not going to hear the end of that sentence.)

"Louie, remember the time we *did* go home after that place in Amherst closed, and we took the girls with us?"

"You mean the night the bed 'accidentally' caught fire?"

Now, if you had been me, wouldn't you have sat as still as you could so nobody would notice you and you could hear this story? That's what I did. It seems that Winnie and Ginny and Dad and Lou all went to Amherst to a bar they liked. They had a good time and closed the place. Nobody had any money left to go anywhere else

6

and the girls were feeling "real friendly" so my dad and my uncle didn't want to just send them home to their own "lonely little house and let all that affection just go to waste." It was decided that the girls would come home to Dad and Lou's upstairs room and spend the night in comfort and companionship, then sneak out about five A.M. before anyone got up. In order to pull this whole thing off, an insider was needed, someone already in the house who could help all the sneaks sneak and not get caught— a lookout...a sister. There were three sisters abiding in those fields: Jewel, Elizabeth, and Marie. Jewel was a quiet, sweet girl. She was intelligent and well-behaved and would never participate in either of her brothers' rowdy behavior. Elizabeth was the oldest and the largest person in the family and would just as soon knock the boys on their asses as look at them for any of their mischief. Marie was her brothers' angel. She was one of the best things any young woman could ever, ever be: a good sport. She was a little gullible, a little free-spirited, a little gutsy, and adored her wayward brothers with the blindest eye ever bestowed on a sibling. So, it was Marie who would be enlisted in this adventure.

Lou called home, got Marie on the telephone, and told her, "Look, Sis, Jackie and I been drinking kind of late. We have two ladies here who are going to be locked out of their own house because of us. We just can't let that happen, can we? We figure we'll bring them on home, they can stay in our room for the night, we'll sneak them out in the morning, and they can tell their mother that they spent the night with you. OK?"

"Where are they going to sleep, Louie?" my aunt asked him.

"In our room. We got two beds."

"Where will you and Jackie sleep, then?"

"We'll sleep on the floor in there—to make sure the girls don't get scared."

(Aunt Marie said that she told Lou, "That's bullshit, Louie, but come on home with them anyway." Lou said that she bought the whole thing and said, "That's a good idea. I'll cover for you." Whichever it was, the plan was ON.)

The guys got home with their dates. Marie had unlocked the front door and everybody got up the stairs without too much noise. When they got into the room, they saw that Marie had put two candles on the dresser for them so they wouldn't have to turn on the lights and wake up the rest of the house.

All was well. Everyone got comfortable, took off clothes, and got into bed. The guys put the candles next to the bed in case anybody had to get up to use the bathroom. But "when the cuddling started" (as Dad delicately put it), they shoved the lit candles under the beds to make it nice and dark. About four in the morning the ominous smell of smoke had drifted down the hallway and into my Aunt Marie's bedroom. She woke up and, being the intelligent lady she was, knew immediately where to look for the source of the smoke. She got out of bed very quickly, ran down the hall to the "boys' room," where both mattresses were smouldering, about to burst into flame. Knowing exactly the right thing to do has always been my aunt's forte. She began screaming her head off: *"Fire! Wake Up! Wake Up! Fire!"*

The frolicking foursome did indeed wake up.

"Get some water quick!" hollered my Uncle Lou.

"Water! Hurry, Marie!" yelled my father. Marie ran to the bathroom—the nearest water supply—looking for something to carry water in.

"Marie, goddammit! Hurry! One of the mattresses is on fire! Get in here quick!"

My aunt ran back into her room and came out with the only thing she had to carry water in—her teacup. She ran into the bathroom, filled the teacup with water and ran into the bedroom with it. She poured the water on one of the mattresses, ran back into the bathroom, filled it again, and ran back into the bedroom to pour the water on the other mattress. Again and again and again she ran back and forth with that teacup full of water while the twins got into their clothes and escaped out the front door and her two brothers stood in the middle of the room

8

laughing too hard to move. "There she was," said my dad, "still in her nightgown, running back and forth, screaming, 'FIRE! FIRE! *Do* something, you goddam fools! Do something! Call the fire department! Wake Dad up! Stop that goddam laughing and *Do Something!*' and trying to put the fire out with the six or eight tablespoons of water in that teacup. Christ! It was the funniest damn thing I ever saw! Women! I love women!"

That's how that particular story always ended—with Dad and Uncle Lou and Aunt Marie and the rest of us laughing until tears came and Daddy talking about how he loved women. It took a lot of years for me to understand what he meant.

I think the thing I really remember is the laughing. That kind of laughing was the most comfortable kind of exercise I can ever remember anyone having. It seemed like love and women and no money and strikes and broken bones and little emergencies were all handleable if there was enough laughing and mock anger and beer to go along with them.

I'll tell you a story that has several of the things I just named in it; you probably know a hundred stories like it. Well, you do if you come from a family of working people whose salaries never quite stretched far enough and who had to have terrific senses of humor to get through.

During one of the strikes my father was involved in, he was out on the picket line. A picket line is a mild-mannered thing now, but it used to be pretty dangerous; people on both sides got mad a lot and yelled ugly things at each other—often *threw* ugly things at each other. Well, my father was walking one, had been on it a few days, when one of his buddies got knocked on the head with a rock and was put out of commission. The guy had a real strong commitment to the union, just like my dad did, so he sent his girlfriend to fill in for him while he was resting up from having his head broken. This woman came to the picket line, sign in hand, ready to march along with Dad and take whatever was going to come. She didn't think there was anything odd about doing that and neither did my dad; with him, *anything* anybody did for the union was the right thing to do and, of course, you'd do it if you were a "regular guy," which all the guys my dad knew were, and so were their girlfriends and their wives (sometimes not the same women, if you get my meaning).

They were marching along in a circle when some guy yelled at the picketers, "Hey! You guys hiding behind women now? You letting women do your walking for you? Real men! I say you're a bunch of pansies and fairies!" The picketers had been told a million times not to answer back to hecklers, but they never listened much. Dad yelled the 1949 equivalent of "Fuck you!" and just kept walking.

"And I'll bet the little lady is a dyke!" the guy yelled back.

"Don't pay any attention, Jack. You'll just be giving the guy what he wants," said the lady.

Dad kept walking. I guess the guy had heckled them for a hell of a long time when he finally got tired of hollering and threw a rock. The rock missed my father, but it hit the lady.

"That hurt, you bastard! Cut it out!"

"Go home to your girlfriend, you dyke!" yelled the heckler.

Lucy (her name) took that one hard. "Listen, you sonofabitch," she yelled, "for your information my old man is named Frank Lepke. He's six feet tall and weighs two hundred and thirty pounds and he'll kick your stupid butt all over the steel mill when this thing is over!"

"Oh yeah?" the guy yelled back. "Well, I know Frank Lepke and he's a six-foot, two-hundred-thirty-pound fairy who couldn't even find someone's butt to kick it."

That did it. I guess it was OK to call her names and my father names and the union names, but it was *not* OK to call her Frank names.

My father described it later like this: "A goddam mountain lion came out of that woman. She went after him like you never saw before. First she scratched, then she bit, then she took off her goddam shoe and started putting holes in the guy with it. Hell! I just let her go at it—she was winning and he was looking real bad, so I kind of stayed out of it. I guess somebody must have called the cops, because I heard sirens and I said 'Lucy, we better get the hell out of here before they get you for attempted murder.' She said 'OK, Jack. Let me get my shoe on.' That's when all hell really broke loose. She started to put her shoe on and then she yelled, 'Goddam it! Godstinkindammit! I got a goddam run in my goddamn stockings! You asshole, you sonofabitch, you filthy bastard!' And, Christ! I thought she really was going to kill that guy. She took that shoe off again and went for him. It took me and two other guys to get her off him and into a car and out of there. I'm telling you, that guy was one mess. I think she might've tore his nose in half and I know she broke one of his pinky fingers. They had an ambulance come get him finally. Jesus! She was all right, calming down, until she got a look at her stocking. I never saw anything like that in my life. Women! God, I love women!"

He meant it, too.

3

About Boxcars
and Connections to Seattle

During the Depression years, my father and his brother Lou worked at a lot of different jobs. To hear them tell it, every job was a gem. I liked the stories about those years because they always seemed to have somebody in them who either saved Dad's "lucky Hungarian ass," or "got that goddam Louie out of there before all of us got killed." Not too long before the war started, in 1941, my Uncle Lou heard that the government was hiring guys to lay pipe in Seattle. He heard that the pay was good, the meals were free, and the women in Seattle had a "friendly and cooperative attitude." This seemed like everything any man could ever want or need, so my father agreed that they should go seek their fortunes in Seattle. The times being what they were, there was a difficulty about getting to Seattle at all, but the Reisz Brothers being what *they* were, nothing was impossible. It was decided with the help of a few beers and twenty or thirty of their closest friends that the best way to get to Seattle was by rail. The Reisz Brothers had only to jump into the empty boxcar of a slow-moving train headed in the right direction and they'd be in Seattle in no time at all.

What do you know about boxcars? Very little, I'll bet. They aren't a major area of interest to the average person. They have dull paint jobs, for one thing. When you're sitting at one of those guard rails, waiting for the train to go by, what generally catches your interest? Two things: the engine and the caboose. The engine, because it has an intriguing shape and it pulls all those cars and the engineer is there and you picture it like a giant cockpit with dials and levers and buttons. You look at the caboose because it's red and usually somebody is in it. But boxcars—boxcars are just big, dirty rectangles with wheels and they're the things you hope there aren't too many of so that you can get going. See, if the train was made up of all engines and cabooses, you wouldn't think that way; you'd sit behind the wheel and just smile and wave at all the engineers and the caboosemen and think what a happy little break in your day it was. But with the boxcars in there, you get bored quickly with watching the train.

Well, the way I heard it was like this: Boxcars are OK. In the days when there was no money for a guy to get anywhere on any kind of transportation, the boxcar was a great way to go. The first thing my father and my uncle did was to find a train going their way>>>>Seattle. Then, they went to the depot, waited for the train to slow down on its way past the station, ran along next to the train, grabbed the handle on the door, and swung themselves up into the boxcar "where," said my father, "you might find just about anything or anybody waiting for you. There might be three or four friendly hoboes—"

"Three or four *un*friendly hoboes is more like it," interrupted my Uncle Lou.

"—or a couple of young kids running away from home, or an escaped convict—"

"Or," my uncle always interrupted again here, "a hot

13

little brunette from Newark, New Jersey, running away from a big, mean husband."

I want to tell you this story from my uncle's point of view because he's the only one I ever heard tell it. Every time it came up, my father got quiet; he didn't laugh real loud or interrupt with a lot of jokes. He'd just get quiet, smile privately—you know, the same kind of smile people get when you ask who was the first man/woman they ever were in love with—my father would smile like that whenever this story came up.

When my father and my uncle jumped up onto the boxcar that was going to take them to Seattle, it looked empty. They got in and found themselves a dry, not-too-dirty corner and sat down to wait for their eyes to get used to the dark and, all of a sudden, there she was. Over in another corner of this boxcar was a woman. My uncle said that maybe that didn't seem too unusual now because "Now there's a woman or two every place you look—even in the men's john sometimes, but back then women just didn't hop boxcars. So I was damned surprised to see her there." This was, according to Lou, one of the prettiest women he'd seen in a long time and he said my father must have thought so too because, when Dad saw this girl, "He looked like he'd just found a million bucks. He just kept grinning and grinning."

"Who are you?" my uncle asked.

"Helen," she said, "from New Jersey."

"This is my brother Jacky," said Lou. Then he got real smart-alecky. "He grins like that because he's deaf and dumb, can't say a word. He's been like that ever since we got on this boxcar ten minutes ago. What the hell's the matter with you, Jack?"

The girl was laughing and my father was laughing until finally he said hello to her.

"What's your name?" asked my father.

"I said, *Helen.*"

"Pretty name," said my father.

"Thanks," said Helen, "what's yours?"

"Jack, like Lou said."

"Suits you," said Helen and my uncle said that, right

then, he could tell they didn't need anybody else in that conversation so he went back to his corner of the car and went to sleep. Every now and then he'd wake up and hear the two of them talking. He said he heard my father tell that girl things he *knew* Dad never told anybody before in his life. He told her how bad he felt not being able to join the army because of broken eardrums and how much he liked working in a steel mill and how worried he was about his mother being so sick all the time and how much he loved his sister Marie and his brother Lou ("That crazy sonofabitch over there") and how someday he was going to have something—his own house and money in his pocket. My uncle said he figured sooner or later that girl was going to get tired of listening, but she didn't. She just sat there with her arms around her knees and listened and smiled and nodded. Then she talked: told about her husband smacking her around—"No serious beatings, you understand, but I didn't like it anyways"—told about the baby she lost and how she cried for a month about it, told about what a dirty town Newark was and how it made her feel trapped to live in a big city, told about how she was going to live on a little farm sometime and have one or two cows and a couple of chickens and a rooster and a lot of dogs and cats, told about how she got married too young to finish high school but she was going to get her diploma if that was the last thing she ever did.

Uncle Lou said that the last time he opened his eyes and looked over at the two of them, Helen had her head on Dad's lap and his one and only jacket was over her, and Dad had his arm around her shoulders and they were both asleep.

Lou woke up when the train stopped. My father was awake and it was light outside; just the two of them were in the car. "Where'd Helen go?" asked my uncle.

"This was as far as she wanted to go," said my father.

The train started up again in a while and neither my father or my uncle said a word to each other for hours. "Seemed like a hundred goddam years of silence," my uncle said every time he got to this part of the story. "Jacky sat there looking at all the scenery going by for most of the day. Finally, he says to me right out of the blue, 'Louie, I almost got off the train with her.' Then he didn't say anything else until that night when we bought a bottle off some guys at a depot and we got real blotto and we were laughing about a fight we got in back in Lorain and how we had to hide in boxes in the alley so we wouldn't get killed by Little Joe Barazelli and his three brothers for calling them Wops. We were laughing and remembering other bars and other fights and then Jacky said, 'Goddam, Louie! A man's got to watch himself with women. I almost got off that goddam train with her and I didn't even know her last name.' We laughed about that for a while, then I said, 'Aren't you glad you didn't, Jack? Hell, you'd've never seen Seattle. Aren't you glad?' And Jacky kind of quit laughing and he got real quiet for a minute, then he said, 'I guess so, Louie. I guess so.' Everything got back to normal after that and we went on to Seattle, where we lived at the Y until we couldn't take the fleas another minute and then we moved in with a family who rented us a room and— Damn! I could tell you some stories about that that would curl your hair. The people we lived with had three daughters and a son and those girls..." My mother never liked the boxcar story anyway so, when Uncle Lou and Dad started to talk about Seattle, she had usually had enough and would drag me into the kitchen to start dinner or something.

The thing was, I have wondered about that boxcar and that girl for a long time. I wonder about meeting somebody and all of a sudden telling them things you never told anybody in your life and that person turning around and telling you the same kinds of things. And I wonder what would happen if you *didn't* let that person get off the boxcar alone or leave the restaurant where you've been sitting or the bus station where you both have been waiting for a bus. I don't know...it's just something I wonder about.

I won't try to fill in the holes in the little bit I know about the three daughters in Seattle. I only heard pieces of those tales and I'd have to make up the rest, which would never be as good as what really happened. But something I did hear about that happened in Seattle always struck me as being part of the Helen story because it came to a similar kind of end.

My father and my uncle worked in Seattle for a while and then heard that PG&E was hiring guys to lay pipe in San Francisco. The pay was better than what they were making and the three daughters, as my father put it, "were making our lives pretty exhausting," so they got on a bus and went to San Francisco. The drinking, the women, and the work were terrific.

My father always *liked* to work. He really did. This is what he said about laying PG&E pipe in San Francisco: "It was real good work. You got up about five in the morning and had some coffee and maybe something to eat with it, maybe not. You got down to the site about six and started putting pipe together, started guiding pipe down into the trenches that the other guys dug. The crane would pick up these giant pieces of pipe and swing 'em around and everybody would be shouting and getting out of the way except for the guy doing the guiding—me and Lou both did guiding—then you'd unhook the pipe off the crane and go to the next piece to get it ready for laying. Sometimes you'd be so tired you wouldn't know which end was up; you'd stop for lunch, which was—every single day I was there—cold meatloaf sandwiches on white bread, and you'd never want to get up again except that all the other guys got up, so you did too and laid some more pipe until about six and then knock off. We'd go home and lay down on cots, which we paid ten dollars a week for, and figure we were never going to get off of them except that we got hungry for dinner, which was usually something with macaroni in it, and then somebody almost always had a bottle and a couple of girls who wanted to go out so we'd pull ourselves together and do it—go out like dumb jackasses until one or two in the morning. It was good work —I'd do it all again in a minute. Me and Lou worked good together, never a fight, always laughing and carrying on. I'd of probably done it forever if..."

Now, the "if" is kind of the start and the end of the

whole story. My Uncle Louie had gotten his seaman's papers a couple of years previous to this Seattle adventure. He was not like my father—the kind of man who could work at something forever if he liked it. Louie stopped liking it, whatever it happened to be, just a few months into it and was always ready to do something else. There was always a better-paying job, a better climate, a prettier woman just across the highway or just one state line over or just across the world. And that's what happened. Uncle Lou got tired of laying pipe, and shoveling dirt, and eating cold meatloaf sandwiches, and he started thinking about all those other jobs and climates and women and where he might find them. He finally decided on the Orient and on the freighter he'd take there.

After work one night, Lou and my father were lying on their cots and Lou said, "Remember that Helen, Jacky, the one who got off the boxcar?"

"Yeah, I remember," my father said.

"Well, I'm going to do that same thing. This is as far as I want to go with this job. I'm getting off this boxcar and getting on another one going someplace else."

"Where you going, Louie?"

"The Orient, Jacky. I'm getting on a freighter and heading for the Orient. They got jobs that pay a lot of money—American dollars, too—and you don't pay taxes on it. They got people there from all over the world—and women! Jack, they got women in the Orient that do it sidewise!"

"Bullshit, Lou!" said my father. "Nobody does it sideways."

"Oriental women do. And they walk on your back and feed you with chopsticks and you can get a drink there for a dime at any bar anywhere. An American gets treated like a king there, Jack, and I'm going. Why don't you come with me? We'll tear through that place like they never saw before, the two of us."

My father thought about it for a little while. "I don't have seaman's papers is the first thing. The second thing is I like it here, Lou. I like the work and I like the guys and I don't care if I ever do it sideways and the money's not bad and neither is the food. I don't want to go anywhere." My father said both of them were lying there, blowing cigarette smoke at the ceiling and thinking about what to say next.

Finally, Lou, who always was the talker, said. "Remember that time in Cleveland when that sailor was going to tear my arms off and you set the cuffs of his pants on fire?"

"Yeah, I remember," said my father.

"And that time in Amherst when that farmer hit me in the head and you jumped on his back and rode him all over the bar?"

"Jesus, yes!" said my father.

"Remember the time that Gloria wrote Ma a letter saying she was pregnant and one of us was the father and you wrote Ma a letter saying, 'Dear Mrs. Reisz, You will be getting a letter from a girl named Gloria who says one of your boys got her pregnant. Well, I'm her roommate and she's a liar'?"

"Yeah, Louie, I remember that." They were both quiet for a while.

"I love you, Jacky," said my Uncle Lou. "I'd love you even if you weren't my brother, but I've always been glad you are. I'm going to the Orient, but I'll be back and we'll raise some hell together again before it's all over."

And he went...and he was...and they did.

4

My Uncle Louie's Bimbo

Now, I'm going to tell you about a thing that happened to my Uncle Louie in New Orleans. I heard this story when my Uncle Lou and Aunt Margie came to visit us. They lived in Louisiana—Shreveport, I think—and came to California twice to visit us. My uncle worked for a newspaper, had been a journalist all his life—a good one, too. Anyway, I heard this story the first time they came to see us. My father is the one who told it, after he'd had three or four beers, over the truly panicky protestations of my Uncle Louie, who feared for his marriage and his life.

"Jacky," he said, "please don't tell this one on me. I'll have to sleep in the yard tonight if you do." My Aunt Margie was about 5 feet tall, about 93 pounds, and meaner than a Tasmanian Devil when she got mad, which she did easily.

"Louie," my father laughed, "you have given me many nights in the yard because you told my wife stories about me. I think it's time I returned the favor." My uncle put his face in his hands and moaned. "Well," said my father, "Louie had always wanted to live in New Orleans. He'd been there once and liked the look of the place. First of all, it was mostly bars and hoochie-coochie places which he liked *very* much as a young man—"

"Oh God, Jacky, I am as good as dead!"

"—and second, the town was full of the prettiest women you ever saw, right, Lou? They were not only pretty, Lou told me, but they had a very relaxed attitude about things, if you get my meaning. They were... let's see, uh, cooperative...friendly...generous...all the things Louie prized in a woman. Lou thought New Orleans must be heaven, second only to Japan, which he told me could not be described but had to be experienced to be believed [another moan here from my poor uncle], so he packed his bags and went to New Orleans to live for a while. There was one bar in particular called the Butterfly Bar and Grille which was Louie's favorite. The drinks were cheap and the gals who came in were friendly and didn't usually try to take a guy for his last red cent. They had a little jazz band and a couple of dancers who were real good—real 'loose' is the word I think ol' Louie used. And one of these dancers sort of got sweet on Lou. Well, hell, he used to be good-looking in those days, at least the women thought so, and he was always jokin' around and foolin' around and making everybody laugh. Women fell in love with him all the time. He was a pretty good dancer, too, and when he had money on him, he was no cheapskate. He'd show a girl a real good time. Louie, re-member that time you paid for that girl's train fare to Cleveland, just so she'd go along with you and, when you got there, she ditched you? I'll never forget that. You were so damn mad....Nobody—I mean, *nobody*—ever ditched Louie. He was so mad, he—"

"You're killing me, Jacky. I swear to God, you're kill-ing me."

"OK, OK. So anyway, there was this dancer who kind of fell in love with Louie. He'd go in there almost every night and wait for her to finish work and then they'd go get something to eat and maybe hit some more all-night joints, then they'd go up to her place and...I don't know ...talk or something. I don't know, what *did* you two do, Louie? I guess she was a real great-looking gal; he showed me a picture of her once and she had great big—"

"JACK!" My mother's voice.

"—brown eyes and a very pretty smile." Dad winked at me here. "Thing was, she wanted to get out of the entertainment business and get married and settle down and have babies. Those were all things that my dear brother did *not* want, and he had a kind of insurance against that happening. Now, Louie's insurance was that he never told all these women what his real name was. He used to tell them he was me—he'd say his name was 'Jack Reisz' so that, if any of those women ever tried to find him after he left town or left the country or the port or wherever he was, they'd be trying to look up 'Jack Reisz' instead of him and I'd be the one trying to do the explaining. He knew I'd take care of it, too, so that our Ma or Sis [my Aunt Elizabeth] wouldn't find out about it. Anyway, then he'd go off to somewhere else all safe and sound. Well, *this* time, the whole thing backfired. One night they were up at this gal's place, and Louie fell asleep. The girl, I think her name was Frieda, woke up and went to the bathroom or something and couldn't go back to sleep. She sat around for a while, waiting for Sleeping Beauty to wake up and, when he didn't, she got restless and decided to go through his pockets. She took out his wallet and started to look through it. Remember, he told her he was 'Jack Reisz.' So she looked at his driver's license, his social security card, his merchant marine ID, his Starlight Club membership card, and they all said 'Louis Reisz' on them. I'm not saying this girl was dumb or anything like that, but she wasn't long on education and she had more imagination than she had sense, and, when she saw all those cards with 'Louis Reisz' on them, she got it into her head that the man sleeping in her bed at that moment had done something terrible with Mr. Louis Reisz, stolen his wallet, and run away. She realized that the last names were the same, so she figured that the dead Mr. Reisz was probably a relative."

"How come you never told me about this Lou?" Aunt Margie was not smiling. "I never heard this before. I thought you said you'd never been to Louisiana when we first met. Didn't you tell me it was your first visit?"

"Goddam, Louie, did you tell her that? I'll tell you, Margie. He hadn't been to Louisiana in a long time when he first met you. That's because a state policeman told him that if he ever showed his face in Louisiana again, he'd string him up." My uncle was beginning to look glassy-eyed with fear. "Anyway, this Frieda had it all figured out to where Louie was some kind of killer who was probably crazy and might wake up at any time and decide to kill *her* just like he did his relative. So, she put her clothes on, sneaked out the door, and went to find a policeman. Well, she found one all right and he came along with her back to her place where poor old Louie was still asleep. The policeman nearly broke down the door coming in and he woke Louie up and took him down to the station. The worst part of it was that the policeman was an old friend of Frieda's and he hated out-of-towners anyway and was more than willing to believe Frieda's crazy version of what was going on. Louie spent three days in that jailhouse explaining to anybody that would listen what had really happened. 'Just call my brother Jacky at home. He'll tell you who I am. I *am* Louis Reisz. Just call my brother. He'll explain the whole thing.' Finally, somebody did call the house. Elizabeth answered the telephone and, when the police asked her about it, she came upstairs and got me and I talked to them and explained the whole thing. Elizabeth was so mad, she said we should've left him there. It's a damn good thing he came home by way of Madagascar because she was ready to kill him right then."

"What happened to Frieda, Jack?"

"I never saw her again, Margie."

"I didn't ask you, I asked Jacky. What happened to Frieda?"

"Well, Louie left town as soon as they let him out.

23

Evidently, Frieda remembered our address from one of the cards in Louie's wallet or her policeman friend gave it to her or something, because she wrote him a letter about a year later saying she was sorry for all the trouble she caused him and she was really grateful to him because she'd married the cop that originally arrested him and they were expecting a baby. Dumb broad!"

We all started laughing then. The story had the right ending and I was pretty sure that Aunt Margie, though she did not look happy, would not make my uncle sleep in the yard—at least not in our yard—while they were in California.

"So," said Aunt Margie, "do you still have a picture of this Frieda?"

"God no, Honey! I threw that away years ago—right after I showed it to Jacky."

Margie looked like she didn't buy it. "Are you sure of that, Lou, honey? You sure you still don't have a picture of that young lady?"

"Sure as I can be, Sweetheart," said my uncle. "Sure as I can be."

"Well, that's fortunate, isn't it?" she said, and flashed a look at my mother; one of those "there's-gonna-be-trouble-later" looks. "Let's start dinner, Mary. I'm gettin' hungry. We eat a little earlier down South than y'all do." And off they went to the kitchen.

My Uncle Louie waited until he heard the sounds of the refrigerator door opening and the pots and pans coming out of the cupboards. Then, he took out his wallet. He opened it, fumbled around in it for a minute, then gave something to my father. "Take this, Jacky. Quick, take it." My father took it and started to laugh like crazy. "Put it in your goddam pocket, forgodsakes! Cut out the laughing—she'll hear you." My father laughed harder. "Christ! Between the two of us, Jacky, it's a wonder we both aren't dead yet. What'd you have to tell her that story for? What the hell's the matter with you?" And then Louie was laughing, too. Both of them were laughing so hard, the tears were running down their faces.

"What's so funny, I'd like to know?" My aunt was standing in the doorway between the living room and the kitchen.

I was sitting all hunched up to the left and a little behind Dad's rocker. Slicker than frog's hair, he dropped his hand down to where I could reach it and passed me what Uncle Louie had given him. I put it down my shirt front fast before anyone saw, and got up to go down the hall to my bedroom. When I got there, I unbuttoned my shirt to see what Dad had given me. It was an old photograph, kind of blurry, of a blonde lady in a bathing suit. She looked pretty glamorous with a pair of big dark eyes and a very pretty smile. I turned it over. "To Jacky," it said. "Boop-Boop-Be-Doop—Love, Frieda."

After dinner, my father came into my room. "Have you got the picture, Muggsy?"

"Sure," I said.

"Better give it to me quick."

"Can I keep it, Dad? If I hide it really well?"

"What do you want with that dumb picture, Muggs?"

"I don't know," I said. "She's beautiful."

"Honey, she was a *real* bimbo. What would you want with her picture?"

I smiled my most smart-alecky smile, put my hand on my hip, and did Mae West for Dad: "Wel-l-l, Jacky, I only got pictures of *fake* bimbos so far. I'd like a picture of a real one. How about it, Jacky Boy? Whaddaya say?"

My father could never resist a smart-alecky joke. He started laughing hard. "It's yours, Muggsy. If you really want it, it's yours. But forgodsakes hide it somewhere where nobody can find it, at least until after your Uncle Lou and Aunt Margie leave us. You sure are a nutty kid. Good night, Honey."

I hid the picture between the pages of a book that got lost somewhere. I don't think I ever saw it again.

5

Something Significant— Like Getting Married

In 1943, my father was the most sought-after bachelor in Lorain, Ohio. He had managed to elude each and every lady who tried to maneuver him into matrimony. There was many a tearful good-bye at bus terminals, bars, and basketball games (you remember, I mentioned that my father played semi-pro basketball) while some sweet female stood holding Dad's hand as he explained his position.

"It's like this," he'd say. "I'm really no good for a nice gal like yourself. I'd probably end up breaking your heart. I'm sloppy and a no-account. I like to drink too much and I have no ambition whatsoever. I'm going to amount to nothing in the long run." Usually that did the trick. If it didn't, he'd just get Lou or one of his buddies to take the woman aside and tell her that Jack Reisz was a dirty so-and-so, and had bastard children all over the state of Ohio. I don't think that one *ever* failed.

My grandmother worried herself into an early grave

over the fact that my father was still a bachelor at age thirty-six. Bachelorhood was not a thing to be wished for anyway, and the way my father seemed to be going, he'd probably die an early death without a wife to keep him in line. Needless to say, there was some disagreement on this point between my father and his mother. In those days, however, a man respected his mother's wishes, for the most part, and so my father met the daughters of his mother's friends, and daughters of second cousins just over from Budapest, and the recently widowed daughters of his father's friends. He remained a bachelor.

My Uncle Lou said that their mother brought over every "knock-kneed, cross-eyed, buck-toothed, skinny [which used to be a bad thing to be], flat-chested, ailing female that ever graced Lorain, trying to marry off Jacky." Still, the thing could not be done. My father wanted no part of marriage... until he met Marcia Dombrowski from across town.

My mother was and is a tall woman—about 5′10″ in her bare feet. In 1943 she was a photocopy of Joan Crawford, the actress. She wore her chestnut hair rolled around and tucked into what they lovingly called a "rat," Joan Crawford style. She was a fine seamstress and wore clothes that looked like they came straight out of fashion magazines, and the highest heels she could find, to accentuate her height. She wore scarlet lipstick and scarlet nail polish to match, and never left the house without a hat. She was and is a profoundly beautiful woman—who didn't much care about getting married to any man in 1943. It seemed to Marcia Dombrowski that getting married would put one heck of a kink in her life; she liked doing things her own way and didn't like anyone, especially some man, telling her what to do. Her brother Joe, with whom she lived, said she was "the damn stubbornist woman" he ever knew in his life. Their parents had died some years before and Marcia was raised by an older sister and brother, both of whom often spoke of Marcia's willfulness. She didn't dress, talk, look, or act the way any other young woman her age in her town acted. These days we'd say she was "her own person." (They said other, less kind things in 1943.)

Anyway, one freezing cold night in January, Jacky Reisz and his crazy brother went to a dance in Amherst, Ohio. It was twenty-five cents to get in and most people brought their own booze in little flasks or small cough syrup bottles, got loaded to the gills, and danced the night away.

Marcia Dombrowski's brother wanted to go to that dance and take his girl, Dorothy. So he took Marcia along, hoping she'd meet some nice Polish boy, fall in love, marry, and have six children the way God intended nice Catholic girls to do. Marcia went along to show off her new purple two-piece suit to "that bunch of farmers in Amherst who probably wouldn't know an actual Paris dress pattern from a housedress."

Off they went. And, it was at that dance that Jacky "Red" Reisz met the lady who was to put an end to his carefree bachelorhood.

They hadn't been at the dance too long when my father noticed Marcia Dombrowski standing against the opposite wall watching the dancers and tapping the toe of her three-inch-heel, brown-and-white spectator pump to the music. My father nudged his brother (according to the most popular version of this story) and said, "Who's that looker over there against the wall? The gal in the purple suit."

"She's too tall for you, Jacky," said my Uncle Lou.

"She's real classy. Got kind of a sassy look to her. Let's go over and introduce ourselves, do the girl a favor, maybe ask her to dance."

"OK by me," said Lou, "but I'm tellin' you, she's too tall for you."

"Well, then, she'll be grateful to be asked to dance," said my father as they walked over to say hello. I've never gotten it quite straight if Mother saw them coming and decided what to say ahead of time, or if she truly was a smarty-mouth lady who could spot a couple of egotistical little snots a mile away. When they got over to her, my father smiled his very best Ronald Coleman smile. "Hi there," he said "I'm—"

"I know who you are and I'm not interested, thanks."

My uncle says that Dad was so unused to hearing such a reaction that he just kept talking.

"—Jack Reisz. I thought you might like to dance."

"No," my mother said.

"Why not? Don't you like to dance?"

"Not with you, hotshot." Mother gave him her coldest Crawford stare.

My father chuckled. "How do you know me, Sweetheart? We've never met."

"No, we haven't'," said Mother, "and guess what? We aren't going to meet. You got a reputation that's followed you clear out to my part of town. I don't even *know* you and I don't like you."

My Uncle Louie started laughing and the two of them walked back to where they came from. "Tall, skinny, smarty-mouth woman. Who does she think she is?" My father was fuming.

"I don't know who she thinks *she* is, but she sure as hell knows who *you* are and she don't want to dance with you." Uncle Louie thought it was pretty hilarious because my father rarely struck out with women. "Boy, did you get the brush-off. I never saw you get the brush-off like you got it this time. She don't even want to dance with you."

Now, if my mother was telling you this story, she'd tell you that my father pestered her day and night after that dance. She'd tell you that he called her house a dozen times a day and had his buddies drive by to tell her good things about Jack Reisz, and that he went so far as to leave a box of candy on her doorstep once with a card that said "Something sweet for something sweet." It was the candy and the card, my mother says, that finally convinced her that one date couldn't hurt and, the next time he called, she said OK, she'd go out with him.

My father says that Mother asked her brother Joe to ask all of his friends to put in a good word for her. My father says that she called his house several times a week to talk to him and kept getting hold of his sisters, who gave him the messages all right, but couldn't make him call her back.

My guess is that somewhere between these two stories is the truth, because they did go out and they did begin dating each other and they did fall...well, sort of fell... well, decided...Here's what eventually happened: In January of 1944, my father got a letter from a guy who'd left Lorain Steel to go to California and open up a new steel mill—Kaiser Steel Fontana. The letter (which you'll see a little later on) offered my father a job if he wanted to come out to California; he did want to do just that. He told his mother and his father that he would like to move to the West Coast for this job and he told his friends he was going. He kissed the girls and shook hands with the guys and drank beers with familiar bartenders in familiar bars.

"Aren't you going to to tell Marcia good-bye? You been seeing her for a while." I think my Uncle Lou was always a little sweet on my mother himself.

"Sure. Sure I am. I'm going over there and see her tomorrow. Poor kid—I told her I was going to break her heart. Now here I am doing it. She's going to be all broken up. I hate to do it, Lou. I'll tell ya, if it's one thing I hate, it's seeing a woman cry. I never could stand that. But, you gotta do what you gotta do, right?"

"Right," said my Uncle Lou.

The next night, Jack "Red" Reisz journeyed to the other side of town to say good-bye to Marcia Dombrowski, who had heard from everyone she knew that he was leaving for California.

I want to stop here for a second and be honest with you. I have heard this story told ten different ways— really. My Uncle Lou, of course, has told it; my father has told it; my mother has told it; my Aunt Lotte and my Aunt Helen have both told it; my Uncle Norby had told it (but he was only about ten when it happened, so I tend to discount his version for the most part). I'm telling you the version I like best. It's my mother's version and I use it because I love the way she grinned with her eyes when she told it. My mother is not much of a grinner, but when she told this story, she looked a little like what you'd imagine a traveling salesman must have looked like when he got out his suitcase of "real gold pocket watches" and grinned through the whole sales pitch. Do you know what I mean? There's fun in it and sort of a little private joke in it and some little bit of demon in my mother's grin. Anyway, that's why I'm telling you her version. I see that grin on her face through the whole story and I like it. Besides, it's the only story she ever sat down to tell. Usually when the stories were being told, she was in the kitchen and would come out to pour coffee or bring a drink to somebody or announce dinner. When this story was being told, she always came out and sat down to make sure it got told correctly.

So, I'm going ahead with the good-bye at Marcia Dombrowski's brother's house. My father got there right after dinner. He was invited in and told to sit down, have a beer, and wait a little because "Marcia had to run a couple of errands. She'll be back in a little while." Dad had a beer and then another one, and she still didn't come in. After he'd been there about an hour, he said, "Joe, is Marcia coming back this evening at all? Did you tell her that I called and was coming over to say good-bye?"

"Sure I did, Jack. She'll be back pretty soon. She just had to go to the store. She knew you were coming. Said she wouldn't be long."

"OK," said my father, "but I can't stay too long. I have to pack and stuff."

After another beer or two, my mother showed up. She came in, said, "Hi, Jack. How've you been? What's new?" and went on up the stairs to comb her hair and repair her makeup. She came back down in a half hour or so and sat across from my father. "Well," she said, "how're things? What have you been doing with yourself?"

Dad by this time was feeling pretty off-balance. Marcia didn't look in the least like she had any idea that he was going away forever, would never see her again. She was examining her nail polish, seemed real concerned over a chip on her thumbnail. "Marcia," he said to her, "I'm leaving next Friday for California. I got a job out there in a new steel mill they're building. I won't be seeing you anymore, but we had a lot of fun together and I wanted to come by and tell you good-bye."

"Hmm," she said. "Well, good-bye, Jack. It's been real nice seeing you." And she stood up to leave.

"Yeah. I won't be back probably. I guess I won't be seeing you again. Just wanted to say..." He sort of drifted off. The thing just wasn't going the way he thought it was going to go at all. She was standing up, not a tear anywhere.

"Right," she said. "I've got a real busy day tomorrow, Jacky. Walter Slomcheck is taking me out to Riverdale for a picnic and a dance, so I'll be saying good night now, if you don't mind. Good-bye and good luck in the future."

Mother has always said that Dad looked right then like he'd tried to swallow a horse whole and couldn't quite get it down. He cleared his throat, he stood up, he sat down, he stood up again. "Marcia," he gurgled, "could we sit down and talk for a few minutes?"

"Sure," she said. "Long as it doesn't take too long, I have a busy day—"

"Yeah, I know, Walter Slomcheck. Listen—do you like me at all?"

"Sure. You're OK."

My father says that he's positive he heard somebody else (because it sure as hell couldn't have been him) say, "Well, uh, I...like you a lot, Marcia. I was wondering if maybe...if you...if you might want to maybe go with me to California."

"What! Are you kidding?"

"No." (Years later when he told this story, Dad said he hoped he might be kidding, but he couldn't stop himself.) "You said you liked me."

"I said you were OK, Jack. There's a difference between thinking you're OK and going to California with you."

"We'd get...I mean...we'd get married first."

"Married. Who's talking about *marrying* you? Where'd you get that idea?"

"I thought...I wouldn't want you to think I'd be taking you to California under false pretenses or something. I'd make it legal and everything."

"I'm not sure I want to marry anyone, Jack Reisz—especially you. First of all, you're too short. You drink too much, you smoke too much, you run around in bad company, you got no romance in you, you're egotistical and stuck up and irresponsible and spoiled to boot. Marry you! I'd be crazy to do that."

Dad said it was the prettiest he ever saw her. He said she was flashing her eyes and her cheeks were red and he wanted to marry her just about more than anything and he hadn't even realized it until then.

"Marcia, you're right about all of that. But, I'm the hardest working sonof—well, the hardest working *man* you'll ever meet. I never quit a job unless I got another one, and I'd never let you go without a roof over your head or clothes on your back. I can't promise about the company I keep because it'll be with who I like to keep it with, but I won't run around with other women if you'll marry me, and I'll try to be more romantic, too. I can't help it that I like to smoke, I'll probably always like a drink or two, but neither of those things will ever keep me from working a full day's work. I'll usually be home on time, I'll hand over my paycheck to you every week, I'll never tell you what to do or what to wear or how to spend what money I make. I'd like it a lot if you'd marry me, Marcia Dombrowski. Hell, I didn't know when I walked in here that I was even going to do this. I didn't know I liked you that much."

Mother was quiet for a long time. Finally, she smiled a little. "Well, you didn't say I was beautiful and you didn't say you loved me. It's not the most romantic proposal I ever heard of..."

"I told you I'd try to do something about the romance stuff. Gimme some time forgodsakes."

"...but you do have some good points about you and you can be a lot of laughs sometimes. I like that. I don't know...maybe I will marry you, Jack. But, I want a nice wedding—not just some hurry-up thing."

"I have to be in California next week to start—"

"You just write to them and tell them you're getting married first and it's going to be a couple weeks. I want time to make a nice suit to get married in and I want some time for a honeymoon, too."

"Aw, Marsh..."

And it's been "Aw, Marsh" ever since. She made her suit and had her wedding and her honeymoon and came to California with him. They took up housekeeping in a small trailer house provided by the company and began the business of caring for each other. My mother says that Dad changed a lot after he calmed down and started being a husband. My father says he never changed a thing except the womanizing and he says that with a look that makes me wonder sometimes. Mother says she probably married way beneath herself, but she felt sorry for him and has probably been the saving of him. Dad says she was so much of a smart-aleck, bad-tempered woman, no one else would've married her, so *he* felt sorry for *her*. They say those things with a tone in their voices that tells you that it was a damn good bargain they both made and that, if it came to it, they'd do the same thing again.

There is a picture in my mind of my mother. She is older now, of course, and is a lovely older lady. But, when I think of her, or have dreams about her, the image I have is always the same one: a tall young woman with fine posture—straight back, straight shoulders—long legs—always wearing stockings, even in the summertime—red-brown hair usually pinned up, dark brown eyes which seemed in some ways secretive, shaded, or guarded somehow, so that the more blatant emotions showed but not the subtler things. I see her in high heels, which she loved to wear, and gloves, and dresses made of fabric that moved easily when she walked. Mother smiled, but did not laugh easily; she was kind and easily moved to tears over things that were sentimental and romantic, but she could be very hard and cold if her wishes were disregarded or if her instructions were willfully disobeyed. I thought she was a very beautiful woman; my father thought so, too. I think he was always a little flattered that such a lovely person would marry him and put so much energy into policing his life and his home. He left all matters of social consequence, education, religion, and money up to her. He said he had no head for such things, that he was just a "working slob" without the faintest idea of how to do things right and that she kept him on the straight and narrow. My guess is that keeping my father on the path of righteousness was no small task, but she has done so for the most part and has been able to keep her gentlewoman's demeanor throughout. There are fewer tall tales about my mother than there are about Dad because she was so much more conservative than he was, but there are a few.

I'm about to tell you one of the best tales my father tells about Mother. Now, there's a reason why he likes this one so much: It's because it points out the hell-raiser that lives deep down inside the lovely, well-dressed, proper Mary that my mother usually is. It has always been important to her to be a *Lady*. I was brought up on five hundred things that a Lady does and does not; some of you were probably raised on the same stuff: A Lady doesn't comb her hair in public. A Lady doesn't check her makeup in a hand mirror in front of anyone. A Lady always has straight seams, never smokes, laughs quietly, eats lightly, looks straight ahead when she walks down the street, always sits with her knees together, writes thank-you notes after the holidays, never cries in public, doesn't fuss with her jewelry or clothing, and never—Never— drinks to excess. Any of this sound familiar to you? Well, Mother didn't just preach those things, she *lived* them and expected me to live them, too. (I'm a middle-aged woman, married twenty-four years, and Mother still asks me every January 1st if I've written my thank-you notes.)

Anyway, this is a thing that happened on my parents' anniversary. I don't know exactly *which* anniversary, but it was a fairly early one because I was just a baby and was being taken care of by my Aunt Jan on the night it happened.

My father had decided to do something special on

35

this particular anniversary. He decided the two of them would go out, somewhere very elegant, and celebrate. The place they chose was elegant indeed: white table-cloths and flowers at the table. The waiter first asked them what they'd like to drink before dinner.

"Cocktails?" he asked.

"Sure," my father said, "we'll have something. What would you like, Honey?"

"I don't know," said my mother, "I'm not sure I ought to have anything. Drinks are so expensive and we—"

"Aw, forgodsakes, Marsh, it's our anniversary. Have something."

"Well, maybe I'll have a highball then."

"No, no. No highballs. You have something special. Have something like Connie drinks." (Connie was my mother's nephew's wife. She was blond and beautiful and had fingernails a foot long. She smoked long *colored* cigarettes and drank fancy drinks with odd names like Side-car, or Dangerous Dan McGrew, or Moscow Mule. My father was always a little sweet on Connie.)

"What should I have? You know I don't drink usually. I don't know what to have."

"Have a Brandy Alexander. I heard Connie say once that they're just like a chocolate milk shake. That sounds real good. Have one of those."

"A Brandy Alexander..." Mother smiled. Visions of Myrna Loy and William Powell moved through her head. She pictured herself in a slim satin gown, seated on a set-tee, a cigarette holder in one hand. The waiter shifted from foot to foot. "Yes," she said, "that's what I'll have."

"A highball for me," said Dad.

When the drinks came, Mother sipped hers. Then she took a bigger sip. Then she took a swallow.

"Like it?" Dad winked at her.

"It's OK," said my mother and finished it off.

"Would you like another one, Honey? It's our anniversary and all..."

"Maybe one more. It's a little warm in here and I'm thirsty."

Dad signaled the waiter and ordered Mother another

one. She didn't even sip the second one; she just gulped it down. Dad offered another. She said yes, then yes to another and another and another.

I need to back up a little here and tell you something important. My father's arm was in a cast on this particular evening. He fractured his wrist somehow. (He said he broke it at work, Little Billy Marshall said he got hit with a pool cue.) So, his arm was in a cast with a sling. He was *not* driving the car. Mother was driving.

At about 8:30, Dad suggested they eat dinner. Mother said "Oh, to hell with dinner."

At 9:00, Dad suggested that they eat *something*, even if it was just a sandwich. Mother said, "I hate eating. I hate sandwiches. I'd rather just have another one of these watchamacallits and watch everyone else eat."

At 10:00, Dad suggested a cup of coffee. The waiter suggested they leave—the restaurant was closing. Mother said she'd be happy to go after just one more whatchamacallit. When the waiter said no, it was closing time, Mother called him a "booger face" and picked up her purse to leave.

"Let's go, Jack," she said. "I'm ready to go home now. This place is"—she arched her eyebrow in what she thought must be a Myrna Loy sort of gesture—"boring."

Dad paid the bill and they walked out to the car. Dad's first clue to the extent of Mother's inebriation came at the moment in the parking lot when Mother couldn't decide which of the four cars left was theirs. She knew it was black and had rope on the passenger side door handle, but she didn't seem to care too much how soon they found it. Mother stood some distance away from the cars.

"Jack," she said, "let's see if we can decide from here which car is ours."

"I *know* which car is ours, Honey. Let's just go get into it and drive on home."

"We will, we will. But let's just see if we can find the car after we play a little game."

"What little game? We really should go home, Marsh. Aren't you getting cold?" Dad was a little uneasy; he hadn't seen Mother quite so *relaxed* before. "I think you

37

could catch a cold out here. Maybe we ought to just go on over here to the car and—"

"No, here's what we'll do. We'll turn around three times with our eyes closed and then we'll see if we can walk right to the car. OK? Let's try it." And she began to turn around with her arms outstretched. She turned around a couple of times and stopped. "O-o-o-o that's fun," she said, and sat down on the concrete.

Poor Dad. He had no idea what to do, so he sat down with her. He put his arm around her and said, "Mary, Honey. We have to go get the baby and go home. You'll want to get up early tomorrow and you won't feel like it if you don't get some sleep. Now come on. Let's go to the car and go on home."

Mother laughed. "OK, let's go, Jack. But you have to find the car first. Bet you can't."

"Bet I can. Come on." He took Mother's arm and off they went to the car. My father says that he was a little concerned about Mother having to be the one to drive in her condition, but that she'd always been the better driver between them and he'd had a few drinks himself so he didn't have the good sense to be as worried as he ought to have been. They got in the car, Mother behind the wheel, and started the engine. "You can drive all right, Marsh?" Dad asked.

"Of course I can drive all right. Don't you worry. I can drive just fine." And she put the car in gear.

You probably know what a crying jag is, right? Too many drinks make some people sad and they start crying and can't stop. Well, it seems that putting the car in gear and starting out the circular parking lot of the restaurant gave my mother a laughing jag. She started to follow the exit signs, which meant she had to make a couple of right turns to get out of the parking lot. Those two right turns must have triggered a tickle someplace because she started laughing and, while she was laughing, she just kept making right turns. Around and around the parking lot they went, Mother laughing harder and harder and Dad beginning to laugh, too.

38

"Marsh, we're not going anywhere," Dad said. "You're driving in circles. We'll never get home this way." He really started laughing. "We'll be here until we're sixty years old, driving in circles. Marti will forget us, they'll give my job to somebody else, they'll repossess the house, and here we'll be, just driving around."

"Oh, Jack." Mother was practically choking, she was laughing so hard. "I might be a little drunk, I think. Mostly, though, I'm lost. We're lost for sure. I think this parking lot has a trick exit or something."

They finally had to stop the car. Dad says that it took them fifteen minutes or so to calm down. He told Mother that he was having more fun than he could remember in a long time. He says now that it was one of the few times he ever saw Mother forget herself like that. Anyway, they calmed down some and decided that they really did have to find the way out.

"I think the way out is over there, Honey." My dad pointed to the farthest, darkest part of the parking lot. "Over in that east corner there," he said. She drove over to where he showed her.

"This isn't the way out," she said, still giggling. She turned off the engine and sat for a second. "I'll just collect myself and we'll try it again."

My father says that she looked so pretty right then. Her hair was up and she was wearing a real pretty cologne. She had made herself a new brown dress with a white lace collar and she was wearing the high-heeled pumps he liked her to wear. Her cheeks were really flushed and she was laughing and smiling all over the place and Dad says he just felt like he had to kiss her right there in the car in the parking lot even if it was outside and sort of in public, which she did not think was very ladylike. But he couldn't help himself; he just put his good arm around her and kissed her ("A great big wet juicy one, which is the way your mom likes 'em").

"Happy anniversary, Mary," he said. And, you know, the drinks and the dark and the occasion and all that laughing must have unhinged Mother a little, because she put her arms around Daddy's neck and kissed him right back, public places be damned.

"Happy anniversary to you too, Honey," she said.

Now, when Dad tells this story, he says, "We sat in that car and necked like a couple of teenagers for ninety minutes."

"We pecked at each other for about twenty minutes and then went home," is what Mother says.

"We left Marti at Jan's all night and went home and had a private kind of anniversary party." (Dad always winks when he says this.)

"We most certainly did not. We left Marti at Jan's because it was so late and too cold to take her outside. You have a very vivid imagination, Jack. Your father has always had a very vivid imagination, Marti."

And that's pretty much the end of the story. My mother's face flushes every time Dad tells that story. She protests and tightens up her cheeks and looks disapproving, but she always blushes and her eyes start looking kind of flashy and movie star-ish. And she always starts to fool with her hair a little, even if she's in public, where a lady is never supposed to fool with her hair.

6

Something About Factories

I love factories. I know how crazy that sounds. I'm not supposed to like anything that pumps pollution into the air, makes too much noise, clutters up the countryside as unaesthetic structures, or makes war materials. Can't help it. I get wacky about factories. I went to a factory once where they make beer. It was a clean factory but I liked it a lot anyway. You could smell hops and yeast everywhere; there was more steam than in a sauna and hundreds of huge stainless steel vats...scrubbed so clean. The machinery was all scrubbed like that, too, and *everything* was in motion. Mixers and separators and pasteurizers and bottlers and canners and blowers and the workers were all moving like the Second Coming was on its way. I was at another factory where they made bags: the Silverstein Bag Company. The place was eight stories high with those green-tinted windows that look like shadowed lids on over-made-up ladies; there was some kind of treated sawdust on the floor for the custodians to sweep up and old latrines toward the back of each floor, the kind with the pull chain and the box up high, strong-smelling green soap in plastic bottles over the sink and the sign we've all come to know and love, LAVA SUS MANOS with grafitti written all over it. It was a real universe. I never wanted to leave, but I wasn't supposed to be in there in the first place, so when the guard came, I went along peacefully. Mr. Silverstein's bag company is my second-favorite factory.

There are not too many factory afficionados in this world, for all the reasons I've already mentioned. Those of us who are around keep it pretty quiet. But real Factory Lovers are sensitive individuals indeed. First, they have to be very accepting about dirt. You can't love factories and hate dirt—they're dirty. People who work in factories get dirt on their hands and faces and elbows. Whether it's dusty dirt or metal shavings dirt, or sewing machine oil dirt or flour dust or hops pollen (if that's what brewery workers get on them), it's dirt and, if there isn't any around, it's not a factory. Second, factory afficionados have to be able to appreciate noise— real noise: machinery pumping up and down, whirring, turning in circles, clacking, mixing, conveying, filling up things, drilling things, emptying out other things, people shouting over the machines, dreaming and worrying and crying and planning and thinking and studying while they're working the noisy machines. Third, anybody who likes factories has to like movement, motion of the most unpeaceful kind. I mean, my God! It's like rock and roll: Everybody, everything has something to do. The machines make the music, the dancers dance. Pull this, push that thing in there, fill that opening, work the lever that opens that up, turn the knob on the right, sew up that eleven-mile-long seam, shovel in the slag when the door opens, push the red button when the light comes on, push the blue button when it goes off, weld this to that, hit the glue gun. Sometimes they have real music going on with all of this. It's practically planetary—the music of the spheres—nothing still, nothing ever really stationary. ANYWAY, that's enough about people who love factories because I want you to know about my first-favorite factory.

In 1943, Kaiser Steel, Fontana, California, opened up. My father was one of the first fifty guys hired out there. He was in Ohio and got a letter (which I'm going to reproduce here for you because I like it) and he said yes, talked my mother into marrying him, and moved himself and my mother out to Fontana where he began as a millwright on the Open Hearth, a job he *loved*, and I mean *loved*, for thirty-five years.

April 22, 1943

Mr. Jack Reitz [misspelling]
1756 E. 29th St.
Lorain, Ohio

Dear Jack:

Received your letter today and am very glad to hear that you want to come out to Fontana and work with us. We will hold the millwright job for you until you arrive.

In regards to your citizenship [remember, I told you Dad was born in Hungary], *we will accept you as one of us. No proof is necessary here.* [I really like that sentence.]

I must admit that finding a house or apartment close to the plant is rather difficult as the plant is about four miles from Fontana proper.

I know it will be impossible for you to obtain a release from the National Tube Company so my advice is to just quit and get your time and go to the War Manpower Commission at Lorain and tell them your wife's health necessitates a change of climate. If they refuse to give you an availability slip, don't let it worry you too much. We will get you one here. We expect to get in operation in the next week or two, so I advise that you come out as quickly as possible. Call me at the Open Hearth office as soon as you arrive in Fontana.

Hoping to see you soon, I remain,
Yours truly,

Harold Johnson

KAISER COMPANY, INC.
Iron and Steel Division

7

"Come Out
as Quickly as Possible"

I think this would be a good place to tell you about Fontana where the Kaiser Steel Corporation lived.

I want to talk about the people first. In 1943, Fontana was a town made up of people who were from someplace else. They came mainly from "back East": Pennsylvania, Ohio, Illinois, Indiana, Michigan. They had worked in other mills in those places, not just steel mills either. They had worked in glass factories and breweries and textile mills. They knew what kind of clothes best shed factory dirt and they knew what kinds of things to think about while factory noises obliterated attempts at conversation. Usually, they didn't think too much about finding themselves or upward mobility or if the road to salvation could be found in the getting of a master's degree in psychology. You probably want to know how *I* know what they were thinking about, standing at their machines. Well, these were people who pretty much talked about what they thought. So, after I was old enough to know what was going on, I listened. I heard them: in our living room talking with my father and my mother, in the dime store on Sierra Avenue, where Mother bought her sewing stuff, and where I'd get treated to a dish of ice cream if it was close to payday and not during strike times, at the drugstore and on the sidewalk in front of the secondhand store. People talked about what they thought.

"Jack," Bob Butler would say to my father, "I was thinking about that guy that used to have the locker across from us. Remember that guy? Mexican, maybe, or Filipino guy. Had the two wives. Somebody told me he took *both* those gals back with him wherever he came from and is still married to both of them and has something like sixteen kids. You hear that, too? Anyway, I was thinking about him—what the hell kind of place would let you bring two wives with you when you went back to it? I mean, you'd think the tax people or somebody would get him for that."

"Naw," my father would say. "I remember the guy, but nobody cares in those countries how many wives you got. I was thinking about him, too. He knew more jokes than anybody. That guy always had a new joke for you."

We would see some man at the drugstore, somebody my father worked with, and he'd say to my mother, "Mary! I'll be damned. I was thinking about you the other day. I ate lunch with Jack and he said you had a cold and I told him about this salve that my Dorothy sells that's for colds and stuff. It's real good—funny color, though—black. Call her if you want some. I got to thinking about the color of that salve, why it's black like that. You ever heard of it, Mary? I can't remember the name of it, but it works real good. Black. Huh. I'll tell you, I couldn't figure out the reason for it being black to save my life. Thought about it all day the day after she brought it home and I still couldn't figure it out." (My mother couldn't either.)

My aunt would call Mother: "Mary. Pat and Frank's girl has polio. I found out Wednesday. Phil came home from work the day he heard it and said he'd been think-

46

ing about it all day and decided no more swimming pool during the summer for the kids, sweaters on them after dark no matter how warm it is, and he wants me to take them to the clinic for *everything* from now on, even if it's just sniffles. He said he just couldn't stop thinking about our girls and what if they got it."

See? That's how I know what people thought about. They said outright what they'd been turning over in their heads all week. They stood in front of those big ovens and shoveled slag and pushed the buttons that made the doors open and close, and pushed the buttons that made the ladle pour and move along the huge track it was on, and pulled the handles that blew the whistles. If it was an election year, they thought about whether they were going to vote the union way or another way. If it was close to payday, they thought about maybe taking the family for a ride someplace and stopping at a fruit stand to buy oranges and nuts. If it was warm weather, they thought about maybe mowing the lawn and asking some chums over for barbecue. If it was the beginning of the week, they thought about "Fibber McGee and Molly" on the radio and if everybody else had heard Jack Benny's latest foolishness.

You can see what kind of people these were. Good people, for the most part. The ones who weren't good knew they weren't and so did everyone else. Somebody was either a "regular guy," or he wasn't. Somebody was either "all right by me," or not. The subject of unhappy childhoods and hidden hostilities didn't enter into it much and a person was held responsible for what he or she was no matter what the reason for their behavior.

"Saw Pete Slotski the other day, Jack."

"Oh yeah? How is he?"

"He looks the same. I never liked that guy. I never liked him even before I found out he beat up his wife and kid. He had a mean mouth on him. Used to say really foul stuff in the offices where the gals are—right in front of them—even when he was sober. I told him once, 'Pete, somebody's gonna close that filthy mouth of yours for you, if you don't watch out.' He didn't listen to nobody, though."

"He never would listen, Andy. That guy got thrown out of Lake's once. Hell, you know Lake's—they put up with anything in that place. But, they threw him out of there because he kept playing with Gloria's ass every time she walked by, finally made her drop a whole bunch of beers. That's when they tossed him out. I told him it served him right, he was lucky nobody knocked the shit out of him. He and I never talked too much after that."

Like I said, these were good people for the most part. They were generally ready to like each other from first meeting. A person had to prove himself bad before anybody would believe it. A group of guys sitting in Domenic's could talk for three hours about what a great human being somebody was. Seriously.

"Bob, you know Charlie Kusack?"

"Christ yes! I know Charlie. He's a hell of a guy. That guy works his ass off, then goes home, cleans up, and takes care of the house and those three kids all by himself. His old lady has that kind of arthritis where you end up in a wheelchair and can't hardly do anything. He does 'most everything for her. Never gripes about it, either. Says she's real smart and reads everything and listens to the radio and tells him about all kinds of stuff. He says he doesn't mind at all that she can't do much because she did it all before she had this arthritis thing."

"He's a good worker, too. Gets his stuff done and helps with yours. Never misses a union meeting, either. And he's right there, passing out food and walking the picket line during strikes. Saturdays, he fixes a lunch, he takes her in that wheelchair and the kids over to the park for the day. Tell you something: he told me once that he was, uh, you know, doin' it with Marilyn over there at the Credit Union. He said he felt kind of bad about it, but he couldn't help it. I told him, I said, 'I don't care, Charlie. You're a regular guy and a real good family man and a good union man and I know your wife probably can't do anything like that anymore. Hell, I'd probably do it to Marilyn myself if I was in your shoes.' He's all right, that Charlie. You can't say nothin' bad about Charlie Kusack to me."

I want you to see what these people were like. They carried with them a built-in readiness to handle whoever and whatever was going to happen. Maybe a psychiatrist or a behavioral scientist would call it a "healthy acceptance level." I don't know what I'd call it. I think it was just something that was issued to them with their undershirts and pleated pants and safety shoes. I think maybe it was brewed into the beer and painted on lunchboxes and poured along with hot liquid steel into the long molded ingots. I think that's were it came from, but I sure don't know to this day what you call it.

Now, the town: Fontana was never a pretty town. It isn't now, for that matter. It was never a veritable garden of clean sidewalks and flowers and blossoming trees. Built on what used to be desert, it was a town that always looked old, even when it was new. The dust that was blown in on the Santa Ana winds stopped in Fontana and never seemed to find any other place to get off to. It settled on the streets and sidewalks, piled up in the gutters, plagued the storefronts, and seemed to find its way into everything except the barbershop which was constantly being swept and cleaned. It just wasn't a pretty town.

During the Fontana summer, everything turned yellow. The sun remembered how a desert was supposed to look and tried to scorch it into shape from July to October. My father's dark-brown hair would sun-bleach out to red, mine would be yellow, Mother would tie hers up like Carole Lombard so that the heat wouldn't dry it out. The newspapers in racks in front of the stores would be yellow by eleven A.M. and the light would bounce yellow off the cement. The union hall was painted with a cheap kind of white paint that sweated yellow drops in the heat. My Dad would say to my mother, "Looks like somebody stood on the roof and peed over the side of the hall there, Marcia." That line was always a good opening for my mother to say something not-so-good about the union. She'd usually say, "Peeing on it is too good for it." Or, she'd say, "If that's the worst thing that anybody ever does to that union hall, I'll be surprised."

My mother was not opposed to the union politically or philosophically. Her opposition was the result of her knowing that much drinking, smoking, and generally rowdy behavior was ever-present at union meetings and that the union was responsible for strikes that meant grocery money would be short, bills would go unpaid, creditors would be angry. She blamed the union for many of the worrisome times of her life.

So, let's see...there was, in the town of Fontana (if memory serves me right), the following: a drugstore, a barber shop, a dime store, a coffee shop, a secondhand store, a bar called Lina's Elbow Room, a bar called The Esquire, a bar called Lake's, a laundry and dry-cleaning establishment called Esquelita's Dry Cleaners and Laundry, a hardware store, and Domenic's Bar. With the exception of Domenic's, those places were on the town's main drag and they were the kinds of places that fit the population just fine. One of my father's friends had a girlfriend—Esther—who told my mother that she loved Fontana because it wasn't "hoity-toity." I promised myself at that moment never to live anywhere that could be called "hoity-toity." Never as long as I lived. I believe I have kept that promise.

The secondhand store was my favorite place. It was a light-brown building with dirty windows. Hand-lettered on one of the windows was this sign: WESCOWITZ ALMOST NEW SHOP—ALL ITEMS AS IS AND IN PRETTY GOOD SHAPE. The lettering was done in orange paint and you could tell that, if Mr. Wescowitz washed the windows, the sign would come off. It smelled old inside, as if the age of all the items in the store—the couches and chairs and books and clothing and tables and lamps—was dusted off daily and ended up on the floor, drying out and giving off a kind of historical odor.

When you walked in, the first thing you noticed was that the walls were covered, floor to ceiling, with pictures. The pictures were all old, of course; some were even framed photographs of people the customers never knew

—or never would know for that matter. Sharing the walls with the pictures were signs: NO SMOKING NO FOOD OR DRINKS ALLOUD ON THE PERMISIS NO ANIMALS ALLOUD RESTROOMS FOR EMPLOYEES ONLY. They didn't apply to me too much: I didn't smoke, my mother didn't allow me to eat between meals, or carry beverages around, I was allergic to animals so I didn't have a pet, and Mother didn't believe in public restrooms. I sometimes wondered who the signs *did* apply to and I always hoped that someone would break the rules—smoke, or eat and drink, or bring in their dog, so that Mr. Wescowitz could holler at them and point at the signs and say, "Can't you read? NO ANIMALS!" It never happened, though.

I was permitted to touch things there. You know how mothers and fathers always tell you, "Don't *touch anything!*"? Well, in the Wescowitz Almost New Shop I could touch anything. They had old chairs and couches and sewing machines and those fantastic framed pictures. There was one of an angel (white, faded greens and blues), who was being kissed on the cheek by a little girl. The picture was called "Mother's in Heaven." I looked at it for at least a half hour every time we went in there. Mother bought it for me after a year or two, saying that she couldn't for the life of her understand what I'd want with such a sad picture. I didn't understand it either. I still have the picture. I still like it. There was another picture they had of a bunch of dogs sitting around a table playing poker. I liked that one, too. My mother said it was cheap-looking so we didn't buy it. I can understand that; nobody could call a picture of an angel "cheap-looking," so it was OK to buy the angel picture. Makes sense.

They also had old clothes there. My mother could sew *anything*. She could sew her own clothes and my clothes and tailor suits for my dad. She could do upholstery. She made me a whole set of bedroom furniture out of upholstered orange crates and it looked beautiful. Sometimes, if she couldn't find the fabric she wanted, she'd go to the secondhand store and pick out a well-made something or other, take it home and remake it. I could look through all the racks and tables and find things I liked and she'd take them home and turn them into brand new things. It was great. They had hats, too—men's and ladies'—mismatched gloves, fancy lingerie (which I was not allowed to buy or touch because Mother said you didn't know where it had been), corsets, pajamas, long johns with the doors on the butt, and shoes. I got to buy a pair of high-top button-up shoes that you put on with a button hook. I had those for a long time before I traded them to a girl named Judy for a stack of contraband movie magazines. I did that when I was eleven years old and I very nearly did not see twelve years old as a result.

The best thing they had at the secondhand store was a used book room. They had turned a very small room into a sort of library. There were shelves all around, all the way up to the ceiling, and books stacked three deep filling every shelf. Someone had penciled FICTION, NONFICTION, TRAVEL on the front of the shelves, but I don't think those labels were very accurate because you could always find Fiction mixed in with Biography mixed in with Travel. I would go into that room, sit down on the floor, and read everything I could get my hands on before we had to leave.

I had been reading since before I turned four years old. That's not bragging, it's just the truth. I had been reading that long for self-preservation. It had to do with boredom. The thing was, my mother did not believe in boredom. So, if I went whining to her on a quiet afternoon, "Mama, I'm bored," she would smile sweetly and say, "Oh, I have *lots* for you to do." I would be given thread to rewind, a kitchen floor to sweep, an apron and a stool to help me do dishes, a dust cloth, etc., etc. I learned to read in order never to be bored and be assigned housework. (Consequently, to this day, I have never been much of a housekeeper and I pity whoever has the misfortune to live with me. I am, however, pretty well-read—a gem of doubtful value.) ANYWAY, I spent a lot of hours in that little room of used books. The floor was tile and stayed cool in the hottest weather. If the place was still there, I would still go there on a too-warm summer day and read until it got cool enough to go back out.

We saw a lot of people we knew at Wescowitz Almost New Shop. Most people bought their husbands' work-clothes there because steel mill men get lots of spark holes in their shirts and pants. You wouldn't want to buy new clothes and have that happen to them, so it was the perfect clothing store for Fontana, and it was the *only* clothing store for a long time. Reba's Ladies' and Children's Wear opened up in 1958, I think. A lot of the women who worked in the Kaiser offices started going there to buy their clothes.

The drugstore was wonderful! It was a clean, white building. The floors were tiled with white, gold-flecked linoleum and inside it looked like the well-stocked bathroom of a very rich family. It was the only store in town with air conditioning—even the bars had only fans —and it smelled nice when you walked in. It had a sign outside that said KOMINSKI'S DRUG STORE OPEN UNTIL 7 EVERY NIGHT BUT SUNDAY in soft blue lights and little handwritten signs next to the cash registers that said WE DO NOT CASH CHECKS. CASH ONLY, PLEASE. Those signs also did not apply to me, as I did not deal with checks, only with cash (in the form of quarters and dimes). It looked fancy, like you should have clean clothes on to go in there.

They had perfume on the first counter you came to and, even though it was a don't-touch-anything store, the lady behind the counter would spray a little perfume on you if you stood quietly with your hands behind your back and looked longingly at the bottles of scent. Usually, my mother bought her cosmetics and her hair accessories and her nail polish and bubble bath and talc and perfume at the dime store. However, the drugstore carried two items that the dime store did not: douche powder and condoms. Now, you need to understand something here. The words "douche" and "condom" were words that were never voiced in my house. I didn't hear those words spoken out loud until I was sixteen years old and in a Senior Problems class in high school. In my house, those words were mouthed silently, or other words were substituted.

53

Watch: "I'm going downtown tomorrow, Jack, do you need *anything?*"

"I don't think so."

"I mean *anything?*"

"No, Hon."

Exasperated sigh. "Jack. Do you need any...you-know-whats?"

"Oh...oh yeah, yeah. You going to the drugstore?"

"Yes."

"Well, just pick me up the you-know-whats when you get your [throat clearing here], uh, stuff."

So, we'd go to the drugstore and Mother would say, "Marti, go over and look at the perfumes and don't touch anything while I go talk to the pharmacist." She'd walk to the back of the store and I'd go stand at the perfume counter and try to look sweet enough to get sprayed with something good. Sometimes three or four people we knew would come in and go back to where Mother was. I guessed that they were all getting the same things and, for a long time, I thought it had something to do with working at the steel mill; everything else did. Once in a while I'd ask Mother what she'd bought there, what was in the bag. She'd say, "Never mind. You'll know when you're older." She never did say what it was. Tell you something, though...I'm forty-four years old and about two years ago I was shopping with Mother and I told her I needed to stop at the drugstore. "For what?" she asked me. "For, uh, some, uh, stuff," I said. "You know, *stuff?*" She laughed so hard, we had to go sit down for a while until she could get hold of herself. Some things just don't change.

The coffee shop was just what you'd think. MORGAN'S EATRITE COFFEE SHOP FRESH DONUTS DAILY was on a sandwich sign that Mr. Morgan put out on the sidewalk every morning. They served BREAKFAST, LUNCH, AND DINNER UNTIL 8:00 P.M., the sign went on. Mrs. Morgan had demanded that the building be painted light green. She had read in her astrology magazine that colors influenced people and that the color green—light grass green—could influence people to spend money. So, light green it

54

was, sort of the color of thin pea soup rather than of grass, but the color made Mrs. Morgan happy. You could smell the coffee from the EatRite even if you were across the street or down the block a little. (It was the disappointment of my life when I realized that coffee didn't taste *anything* like it smelled.) And there were always people in there.

It was a place of handwritten menus, coffee and tea and sodas and ice cream and grilled cheese sandwiches and doughnuts under glass lids. Mostly I ate grilled cheese sandwiches there. I loved them. If my father was along with us, I loved them even better because, when I ordered one, Dad would say, "O-o-o-o, you're gonna have that stinky cheese sandwich again. Oh no!" He hated cheese and he'd make a big fuss, talking about how I must be half mouse or something to eat all that cheese and how the coffee shop baited their mousetraps with that stuff and I better be careful. He'd carry on like that until the waitress would laugh and give us free refills on Cokes. He did the same routine every time and I never got tired of it.

On Saturdays in the coffee shop we often saw the people Dad worked with and they'd holler, "Hey Jack, how ya doin'?" and sometimes they'd come over to the table and talk to us, and sometimes (oh happy day!) they'd invite us over, or invite themselves to our house, or Dad would say, "What are you guys doing tonight? You want to come over?"

They'd say sure, or how 'bout after dinner, and then the party was on. I've loved coffee shops ever since—held them responsible, I think, for the beginnings of a lot of great Saturdays.

The dime store was one of the Wonders of the Western World. I believed with all my heart that a human being could live indefinitely in a dime store and never have to go anywhere else. It was the longest building on the main street and had the most professional-looking sign: NAGY'S FIVE AND DIME—SHOP SMART WITH US was in yellow and pink and purply-blue neon. It looked like a big city sign to me, like a sign you might see in downtown

Los Angeles. (I had not often been to downtown Los Angeles, but I was sure all their signs were neon.) The windows of Nagy's were always being polished so that you could see the displays nice and clear. Every holiday brought on a new display: Christmas was Santa Claus and Mrs. Santa Claus and toys, Easter was rabbits and chicks and fake grass and candy, Halloween was black and orange draped crepe paper and pictures of witches and ghosts. They didn't display anything for the Jewish holidays because I think everyone in Fontana was either Roman Catholic, Methodist, or nothing at that time. Nagy's always looked new, too. So, everytime we went in there, it felt like a grand opening or something.

First of all, they sold popcorn and they sold Cokes and cold sandwiches and pie at the lunch counter. You could live on that. They also had cosmetics, toys, stationery supplies, some clothes, blankets, jewelry; anything needed to sustain human life was sold at the dime store. Fontana people browsed in that store for hours, looking carefully at everything. The purchase of a hair ribbon could result in hours of walking leisurely down aisle after aisle, finally stopping at a counter freshly stocked with boxes of crayons and drawing paper or a rack newly hung with scarves and handkerchiefs. It was a store full of wishes, humble enough that a few of those wishes were possibilities and, on payday, could become realities.

I'm not certain what I can tell you about the bars except that they were dark and cool and as necessary to that town as was the mill. Domenic's was a place unto itself, but the other places had to be just what they were: caves, hiding places, places where—for a little while—a man was in control of his own life. His paycheck allowed him to buy a drink, a smile from a pretty lady, and some conversation with the guys. Afterward, he could go home to cope with bills and kids and car repairs.

The Esquire Bar was a little more high-class than the others. It was a place where the barmaid wore an honest-to-god uniform and wrote your order on a printed tab. You had to get spruced up to go there; it wasn't an after-work kind of place. The outside of the Esquire was mostly black tile, with one darkened window and a pink neon sign that blinked the name on and off. It was small and dark inside and kept cool by a large fan that hung from the ceiling. The juke box looked like what I imagined "The Big Rock Candy Mountain" must look like—big and solid and with bright colored lights moving around the outside of it. It was quiet in the same way a library is quiet and never seemed crowded even when every table and booth and bar stool was filled.

Little Billy Marshall, a friend of Dad's, told him that the girls who sat on the bar stools in the Esquire were the whores and the girls who sat in the booths were just looking for a good time. My father said that's what everybody's looking for—a good time—and doubtless those gals would find it if anybody could.

Lina's Elbow Room was a polka palace. The building itself was big and bright yellow—no windows. The door was propped open from eleven A.M. to two A.M., even in the worst weather, and the music from inside came rolling out like marbles out of a tin box. It was large, with high ceilings and a polished wooden floor that vibrated and thumped with every dance step. Booths were along the walls, no tables, so that there was plenty of room for dancing. They had a juke box with polka music on it, and on the weekends they had a live polka band. The beer was cold and families could come because they served food, too. There were bowls of peanuts on the tables. It was a good summer place. My father used to take us once in a while. I'd eat peanuts and drink ginger ale and watch my mother and father dance. They were pretty good, too. Everybody who got up to dance was pretty good.

Dancing the polka is something that comes with being Polish or Slovenian or German or something similar to those things. If your ancestors came over on the Mayflower, there is a very good chance that you may never, ever really learn to dance the polka. Oh, you can get out there and someone near and dear to you can show you the steps, but it's not the same. It's not the polka the way it's supposed to be done.

First of all you have to like beer. *Cold* beer, not room temperature English ale. You have to like beer enough to drink at least three of them before the band starts. You have to have had something sausage-y and dumplingish to eat, or maybe some sauerkraut or some stuffed cabbage, you know the kind of stuff. In fact, if you were born with a kielbasa (Polish sausage) in your mouth, you've got it made where the polka is concerned. Now, when the band starts, real polka people get up immediately. They don't wait around to see if anybody else is going to dance or not. They don't care. In fact, if nobody else wants to dance, good. That means they have more room. So, they jump up and grab a partner—any partner. It can be a little kid or an old lady or your wife or your younger brother's fiancée. And the person who gets grabbed never says no. The dancing starts. For it to be real polka dancing there has to be hooting as you dance around the corners of the dance floor. Hooting is a requirement—it must come from the women *and* the men. And *you have to sweat.* "If you ain't sweatin', you ain't dancin'." (My Great-Uncle Tony in Ohio, who was well-known for his homemade sausage, was even better known for the way he danced the polka. When he danced, he lost ten pounds just from sweating. He's the one who said that. He told that to my cousin Dorothy's fiancé whose origins were French, and who said to my Great-Uncle Tony, "Boy! You sure do sweat when you dance.") That's how the polka is supposed to be done: with beer and food and hooting and sweating. And that's how it was done in Lina's Elbow Room.

I think we might have gone to the Elbow Room a little more often, but the beer was more expensive there than it was at Domenic's. My father said that that was how they paid for the band. So, my parents only went there when we were flush.

Lake's was a bar for the younger set. The young men needed a place to get loudly drunk and wildly obnoxious. Fights happened and windows got broken. It was down at the very end of the main street and, if it weren't for the big red sign on the roof that said LAKE'S BAR COCKTAILS BEER AND WINE, you wouldn't even know the bar was there. They didn't open the place until five P.M. and, every once in a while, the screen door would open and somebody would fly out, ass over tea kettle, and land on the sidewalk. They usually lay there until the sheriff came to scrape them off the ground and shovel them into the pokey.

The owners, Herb and Minnie Lake, were not too mindful of the law, so they served anybody anytime. It was well-known that they had to hire new barmaids every two weeks or so because the clientele was so rough. My father never went to Lake's, but he liked to tell this story about the place: Little Billy Marshall went in there one night because he was sweet on one of the barmaids and wanted to wait for her to get off work and maybe go out for breakfast at the truck stop. When he walked in the door of the place, the first thing he saw was some big fool with his arm around his girlfriend. The man had backed her up against the bar and was coming on pretty strong. Billy walked up to him and demanded that he leave the girl alone, but the man—underestimating the extent of Billy's rage and Billy's ability to express that rage—said, "Go away, little boy, before you get hurt." And he turned back to the business at hand. Billy walked quietly behind the bar, picked up a pot of hot coffee (which all bars keep on hand), walked around behind the man, and pulled at the waist of his workpants. "Hey, you got something on your pants here," said Billy, and he poured the coffee down the back of the man's pants. Shock and pain gave Billy enough time to run for the door. The man was screaming and shouting and cussing at him. Billy ran out the door, down the block, and into the Elbow Room's men's room. He was so scared that he stayed in that rest room the entire night, and only came out at eleven the next day, when they opened. He was, of course, late for work for the first and only time in his life and, for that blight on his spotless record, he forever blamed Lake's. By the way, he never saw the girl again either. My father loved to say that Billy heard that she married the guy who got the hot coffee poured on him and they moved to Poughkeepsie.

Shakey's Barber Shop was men's territory. It was a little, two-chair shop, all lit up inside and freshly swept at all times. It was Shakey himself who kept the shop "cleaner than a baby's butt" without benefit of a clean-up boy or a cleaning lady. It looked exactly like all barber shops look: red and white barber pole out front, big window, bottles on shelves, shoe shine in the back of the store—you've seen a million of them. This was just one more. It smelled wonderful, looked like a happy place to be in, and was the source for many of the fine jokes my father brought home to us.

Shakey the barber thought that part of the barbering business was knowing and telling jokes to his customers. It went with the hair tonic and witch hazel. He was a tall, thin man with a bald head and a gold tooth. The jokes he told were hilarious and dirty and I never heard one of them from anywhere but inside my room because that's where I always had to go when Dad got home from the barber shop and said, "Shakey told me a good one, Honey. Muggsy, go on back in your room and read something. I want to talk to your Mama kinda privately." I'd go, but I'd sit on the floor in my room—right next to the door—and listen to every single one of those stories. I never could figure out why he always told the jokes to Mother. She almost always got mad at him and at Shakey for telling such "nasty things" to "decent people." I think Dad liked it when she said that. It made him laugh as much as the jokes.

I've always liked the look of barber shops. I think they look friendlier than beauty salons and, in my whole life, I have *never* heard one really good dirty joke from a beauty salon. I would have liked frequenting Shakey's with Dad, but I didn't go because the one time I asked, his friend, Bob Butler, said, "Why, Honey, if you go in there, ol' Shakey will shave your head and make you look like a boy because only boys are supposed to be in there. But you may come along if you want to." I didn't want to. Dad told me later that Bob was only joking and that, if I really wanted to, I could come. But I figured that there was a first time for everything and I didn't want to be the first bald-headed girl at my school. So to be on the safe side, I stayed clear of the place.

Well, that's what Fontana was like. It was a town— wonderful and crummy and small and energetic and real. It was too hot in the summer and not cold enough in the winter and nothing about it to make it memorable to anyone but me. It was built around and because of a factory, a steel-making factory: the Mill.

A steel mill is the finest kind of factory in the world. Nothing is noisier, uglier, hotter, dirtier, faster, meaner, or more beautiful than a real steel-producing steel mill. Everyplace you look, the heads are covered by hard hats and all the overheated, tired feet are in steel-toed boots, and you can tell by looking that the guys shoveling all that stuff into furnaces are wearing skinny-strap undershirts under their workshirts. Look, I know what this sounds like: you're probably thinking that this is some kind of romantic vision, a sort of ode to the working man. Well, it isn't that at all. It's simply part of a picture and will all work into what it's supposed to be as we go along.

Steel mills don't just make noise, they ROAR. If you've ever been in the Lion House at the San Francisco Zoo at feeding time, you'll know what a roar really is. It's thunderous. Everything is alive with it, like an earthquake or a hurricane. The noise is so ferocious that it moves, makes a tornado. I used to think that the Santa Ana was caused by the Kaiser Steel Mill; it made me feel like my father worked in a very powerful place. When you walk through a steel mill, the energy is enough to make a factory afficionado weep. The light and color are something you'll never see anywhere else: there are Ford Mustang yellows, Milky Way candy bar browns, Revlon "Really Red" lipstick reds, baby shoe bronzes, and Xerox Memorywriter blacks. If those escape you, try these: Gauguin yellows, Picasso browns, Warhol reds, Rodin bronzes, and Goya blacks. (Pretty good, huh? I'm not sure which of those descriptive phrases I like best, so I'm going to keep them all in.)

8

Of Smells and Smiles

Smells are funny things. (There's an opening line for you.) At one time we lived not too far from an orange-processing plant in a house blessed with an army of red ants that paraded back and forth in our driveway. My friend Paulette-from-up-the-street and I used to sit in the driveway of that house and watch the ants parade back and forth. We liked to torment the ants a little and would sit quietly poking and prodding them, all the while smelling the orange-processing plant and thinking it was the red ants. So, in my mind, red ants had a tangy, spicy orange scent that was really kind of nice except that the little buggers bit like hell and after a day in the driveway with Paulette and the red ants, my legs looked as if I'd been tortured in some POW camp. That's how it is with smells, though. They aren't always what they're supposed to be. In the evenings, right before the 4–6:30 P.M. breeze died down, strong, significant smells came out of the mill. Sulphur was one, a sort of tar smell was another, a hot metallic smell, like when the car overheats, was another. Mostly, though, it smelled like a gigantic picnic, with the world on the barbecue.

Anyway, about four o'clock I used to start smelling that smell and it meant that it was time to go get my father from work. We'd drive to the entrance/exit and park the car. We'd wait a little and then a wonderful thing would happen. Someplace back behind where I couldn't see, they'd open a gate or a door or several gates and doors and two zillion guys would come out of the mill with their lunchpails and boots and grey work clothes. They'd come out into the parking lot, most of them laughing their heads off, lighting up cigs and *there was this great smell.* It was *them.* The world was not being turned into a shish kebab, nobody's car was overheating, it was all those guys carrying the mill home with them in their lunch buckets (Mother *always* said "lunch buckets") and in their pockets. That's what that smell really was and I have never smelled it since without getting those same butterflies in my stomach that I got then, waiting for my father and my Uncle Phillip to come out with all their buddies and see me by the turnstile waiting and then telling Dad "You got a real pretty girl waitin' for you, Tex." (I have never known why they called my father "Tex," and he says he never knew either, except he thinks it was because some guy had scratched "Tex" on his locker before he got there and made it his locker and they never sanded it off. So guys called him "Tex" unless they knew him really well, then they called him "Jack.")

My father was not a particularly tall man but you could spot him right away. *I* could. He smiled all the time and everybody who was with him smiled, too. He'd come out of that steel mill grinning like he had some kind of terrific secret that he'd be damned if he was going to tell you. Now, I have to stop here and tell you something about my mother. I think it'll say a lot if I tell you how mad that smile of his made her. She used to say he was keeping things from her and that's why he was always grinning. And when he was drunk he smiled like that even more, and she got even madder then. Somehow I'll bet a lot of people's mothers were exactly like that: mad at those secret kind of "ain't-I-havin'-fun-that-you-don't-know-about" smiles, which mainly came from working men's faces after work. My best friend's mother used to throw the newspaper across the room at her husband for smiling like that. She'd say, "May I ask what's so funny?" and he'd usually say "Nothing" and she'd say "Then what are you sitting there grinning at?" and she'd heave the newspaper at him. Of course, my mother would never have done anything like that. She was definitely not a thrower. She did, however, swear like a sailor (in Polish) and bang cupboard doors and pots and pans so hard that your eardrums were apt to fight back. ANYWAY, I was talking about the smiles (right after I talked about the smells—see, that's the poet in me). Well, there were these smiles. I don't see them anymore like I used to. My father wasn't the only one who had one, either; my uncles had them, our neighbors had them, the butcher at our market had one of those smiles (he spoke Spanish almost exclusively, but was "very clean and really knew his meat and seldom tried to cheat you and besides they gave us credit," my mother said), and our mailman had one.

Men didn't have to be blue-collar types to wear one of those smiles. My Uncle Gib—my favorite uncle, so you will hear a lot about him—was an accountant for a private businessmen's club, the Jonathan Club (picture a Hollywood version of the typical Englishman's club and you've got it). Uncle Gib wore suits and ties to work but he still had that smile. I don't know, I think the smile was from the same place they bought those skinny-strap undershirts. I'll bet even Einstein had one of those undershirts. There's probably a photo lying around someplace with him and a neighbor sitting outside with a couple of beers or a glass of schnapps or a glass of wine and they're both wearing those undershirts and those smiles. Undoubtedly, Einstein's secrets behind the smile were a little more cosmic or something, but I'll bet his wife hated it when he smiled like that. I'll bet she hated the neighbor, too. My mother *always* hated the neighbor—or the guys Dad worked with and loved in a way he could never love anybody else.

9

Something About Friends Which Sounds a Little Corny but I Think You'll Like It— Oh, and Something About Floozies, Too

My father had a lot of friends—the kind who would come down and bail you out if you were drunk and disorderly in some bar after a ball game, or would be the alibi you told your wife so she wouldn't be pissed off at you for a flirtation with a floozy that kept you out until six A.M.; the kind of friends who were great poker players because they all lost the same amount every time; the kind who don't care how cheap the whiskey is that you're serving or how old it is—just so they can drink it out of a shot glass and wash it down with a beer, the kind who don't care if you're married and they aren't, who'll bring a date and come to your house on Labor Day for a barbecue even if your wife doesn't care too much for them and they know it and they'll stay until *you* want them to go, which may not be until three A.M. Men used to have those kinds of friends—my father did. Listen to these names: Andy Kushner, Bob Butler, Billy

Marshall (names to remember because these guys were definitely trouble).

Andy Kushner was a little older than my Dad. He'd been married, but he'd been divorced awhile, so he was single. He was not a handsome man, but he had that damn smile and he could drink my father and three other guys under the table and still drive, a feat for which he was highly respected. I heard my father telling my Uncle Phil once that the other thing Andy Kushner could do when he was totally blitzed was "get it up." My mother hollered at that and I didn't know what he meant, but my Uncle Phil allowed as to how that was indeed something to be admired in Andy and thereafter treated him with new respect.

Bob Butler looked like a salesman. He wore white shirts a lot, but that could have been because he was color blind, although the color blindness could have been a lie. One of the things men used to be able to do was to tell little girls outrageous stories and see how long they believed them. Of course, the fun was in believing them forever. Bob wore white shirts and had fourteen girlfriends—all of them floozies, which was what he liked best about them. He brought them to our house whenever he was invited. Bob wore gold-rimmed eyeglasses, which made him look like an intellectual. He was more of a talker than Andy and, while he looked more harmless, my mother said he was five times the trouble of any of the rest of them. He was the worst tease. The first time I met him, I asked my father what he did for a living. Bob started laughing and said he broke off little girls' arms and bopped them over the head with them. I must have looked scared to death because everybody started laughing like crazy and Bob's blond floozy picked me up and said, "Honey, he never broke off nothin' in his life but the seal of a bottle and sometimes *I* have to do that for him. So, don't you worry. Isn't she the cutest thing? Look how serious she looks! I'm gonna *kill* you, Bob Butler!" Then everyone was laughing, even me, because it was a joke and I would not lose my arm and that lady liked me and thought I was "cute" even with my glasses and my too-big front teeth.

Billy Marshall was a little guy. I think he reminded Dad of his brother because he was short but wiry, and could have a bad temper if he was dealing with management, cops, or scabs, or guys who were a whole lot bigger than he was and thought they were smart. I think it was Little Billy Marshall who was right in there with Dad the time he worked the picket line and started turning over the cars of the guys who tried to cross it. I think he was there, too, the time Daddy was going to "poke that goddamn foreman right in his Irish snoot!"

Billy Marshall said, "Next time do it, Jack. I'll be right there to see he don't get up."

Billy was a little guy who liked tall girls. He used to bring over one girl in particular—can't remember her name—who was about 5′10″ and very thin. I know the height because my mother was a tall woman and she was 5′10″. This woman dressed in a kind of classy fashion that appealed very much to Little Billy. She didn't smile much and my father said that that was because one of her front teeth had been knocked out in a somewhat "rowdy altercation at Domenic's" one evening and she was a little embarrassed about smiling and showing that gap and having to explain it to people. I can understand that.

Now I'm going to break the structure of this whole thing again because I just remembered something you should know: My father always said things like "rowdy altercation" when he meant a brawl in the bar or he'd say "we had a few words" instead of saying he and so-and-so were pissed off. The reason for this was that my mother thought it was low class to speak graphically and would call him on it. "*Not* in front of Marti, please, Jack. That's fine for the mill, *not* for the dinner table." Later, Dad and I would go into the living room and I'd say was he really going to poke that guy in his Irish snoot? and Dad would say no, he was really going to kick his Irish ass for him all the way back to Dublin, but Mother better not hear it like that. Sometimes, Dad's friends would loosen up and let fly with some very creative cussing. And, since Mother couldn't very well in all politeness tell them to watch their mouths around her daughter, please, she would spend a lot of time giving me and Dad the Look. It meant: "Marti, you're not hearing this, and you will not remember any of what you're not hearing at this moment." And it meant: "Your friends are lower than fish snot, Jack, and I'll discuss this with you later."

I wanted you to know about this before I went any further because I might forget to tell you later on and it's something I didn't want to leave out.

Now, here's the floozy part. I liked floozies. A lot. Still do. First of all, they always smelled like vanilla, which happens to be one of my favorite smells. Men like it, too. One of the women's magazines says so. Anyway, floozies always smelled like vanilla, and I have spent half a lifetime looking for the perfume that does. The floozies could have won the Pillsbury Bake-Off just walking in the door. Second, they colored their hair. If they wanted to be a blonde, then, by God, blond it was: yellow, haystack, banana, butter, floozie-color blond. If they wanted black, then it was black as ink, black as black cats, black as charcoal, floozie-color black. And, if it was red, then it was hell-won't-have-it red! It was red like a stoplight, or like a crazy sunset, or red like the filling in strawberry pie. It was valiant, I-don't-sweat-you red, floozie red. The very best kind.

Floozies didn't diet, either. They didn't worry about being skinny. They worried about their roots showing or running out of lipstick or whether or not their boyfriends' wives were going to find out, or if they had enough money to go to Domenic's and still get their hair *and* nails done on Saturday. But they didn't worry about being skinny. They'd come to our house with their faces painted on right from the magazines. Every one of them was a Lombard, a Monroe, a Harlow from steel town, and they pranced around in the highest heels they could find and smoothed out their nylon stockings with the softest hands I ever felt. They held out their glasses for more and didn't care if I spilled a little on them when I brought them back filled and they laughed loud enough and long enough to make anybody laugh with them. They'd ask to "play" with my hair, to put it up "like a grown lady," and they'd put a little rouge and lipstick on me. They would unscrew their earrings and kick off their shoes and eat whatever was on the table in front of them. I remember one woman Bob Butler brought over telling Mother that she never dieted because the first place she lost weight was in her boobs and "what earthly good is that?" They worked in the mill offices or waited tables or worked in the movie theaters and went out after work with the millwrights and custodians and slag shovelers from Kaiser Steel. They were "good sports," cartoons, loving art objects, all different and all exactly alike: three-foot fingernails, tight sweaters, tight shirts, and polished lust-colored eye shadow, and, in spite of the fact that I was supposed to grow up with a good education and a teaching position somewhere, I wanted to be a floozie more than anything.

You might be thinking that I'm talking here about whores—I'm not. These women were floozies. *Big difference.* The difference is like the one between being a chef and somebody who just likes to cook. See what I mean? It's important for me to make this point very clear. Because I really wanted to *be* one of those women. I used to see those gals (Dad called them "gals") at Domenic's, which was as fitting a place for them as the church is for born-again Christians.

10

United Steel Workers of America— The Union

I learned early, early on that the way to find out almost anything I really wanted to know, was to BE QUIET; not quiet as in just not saying too much, but quiet as in not saying *anything,* not moving, not twitching, not blinking, not even breathing so anyone would notice. I mean it. One heavy sigh, and it'd be all over.

I remember my dad had the union steward over for dinner one night. They were into a discussion that was giving mother hives and the atmosphere in the living room was beginning to feel a little like the Open Hearth door had just opened up for the slag shovelers. I was sitting on the floor under the piano bench learning how to swear in at least three different languages when my stupid foot went to sleep. I tried to ignore it, but it got those little needles going and I had to move it. That's all it took —I got noticed: "Jack Reisz—Marti is sitting over there hearing every single word you *gentlemen* [this word said

72

with enough ice for skating] are shouting at each other. Now that's *Enough!* Marti, get your bath and go to bed. Say good night to Daddy and *Mister* Grabacz." Evening over. See what I mean? The only way to learn *anything* was to be completely immobile—like a stone. That's the way I found out all about the Union.

The Union was what stood between the amoralcapitalistrichfathead blood-sucking Management Pigs and a decenthardworking Family Man. There were always a lot of other clubs and organizations around for people to join. There was the Masonic Lodge, the Optimist Club, the Chamber of Commerce, the Elks or Moose Lodge, the Mystic Knights of the Clover Leaf, the Shriners—all kinds of groups that sort of stood for something and the members would get cleaned up and go to the meetings and have refreshments after. Or they had dinner dances where everyone dressed in clothes that made them look as if they were at a wedding. They sat at long tables to eat chicken in sauce with peas, then danced to the music of four guys in suits who played an accordion, a piano, and two violins. No beer. They had a lot of class, those organizations, but weren't much fun from what I heard. My Uncle Phillip belonged to the Knights of Columbus, but he said it was just like the Union because "they even let hunkys and Polacks in same as the Union does, long as they're Catholic." I have a feeling my father hated that remark a lot but didn't want to say anything because my Uncle Phillip was married to my mother's baby sister, which gave him immunity from being resented like vaccinations gave you immunity from smallpox.

Back to what I was telling you: The Union was different. It was more like a family than an organization. To begin with, it was *not* voluntary because "Why should a guy get all the goodies if he don't even pay union dues and we bust our asses to get good benefits for ourselves and our buddies and the same guy don't even like the Union?" So, the steel mill was a "closed shop" and Union members were drafted, so to speak, instead of joining up just like in a family (of course, you can marry into one, but then you still aren't *really* in it). Anyway, I don't think

73

most of the guys minded the fact that they had to belong; they wanted to anyway.

Nobody dressed up to go to a union meeting. The guys dressed however they felt the most comfortable. They wore workshirts and workpants and shoes *without* steel toes for a change. They took showers but didn't shave, and didn't put on after-shave lotion, and they didn't follow parliamentary procedure: When they wanted to say something at the meeting they just hollered it out, family-discussion style. There were no "refreshments" after the meeting, either—there was beer on tap and a gigantic coffee urn, nothing else. No "dinner dances," either. The Union had picnics—hot dogs, punch, beer, chips, and it didn't cost a cent. The picnics were a "freebie," my father said, to help the members forget that the union hotshots drove around in Oldsmobiles and Buicks while everybody else was making payments on used Chevys and worrying about the next strike.

I knew four important things about the United Steelworkers of America: 1) They had strikes; 2) They brought my father home happy after the meetings; 3) My mother hated them; and 4) They were like God because you never—repeat, *never*—were permitted to badmouth them.

The first strike I can remember was one that lasted about a month. My father and Andy came back from a union meeting one night talking about "busting management's balls" and singing a song about a woman whose "flamin' red hair did passionate justice to her scanty underwear." I was immediately banished to the bathtub and bed while those two sat in the kitchen recounting the meeting to mother (for their benefit, not hers) and writing down on the back of their last pay envelopes who voted *for* striking and who voted *against* it.

Mother said, "Now, just what are you going to do with that list, may I ask?"

"We're gonna keep it, just to remember who our friends are, Marcia." This from Andy.

"Yeah. Who our friends really are," echoed my father.

"And what about the ones who *aren't* your friends?"

"You worry too much, Honey," said my father. "Where's Marti?"

"I'm in here, Dad!" I shouted that real fast before Mother could say I was asleep; I didn't want to miss anything and, if Dad knew I was still awake, I could get up and get beery kisses and hugs from him and Andy and hear all the stuff that was going on, which is exactly what happened.

There was going to be a strike. My father would be home in the daytime, there'd be a lot of horsing around —teasing Mother, making her mad and making her laugh. There would be walks to the grocery store and visitors in the evening to talk and yell about picket lines and demands and scabs. It was going to be great!

I don't know—it's probably wrong to remember it that way. My mother hated it. She still says it was a bad time that practically gave her a nervous breakdown.

11

Times that May
(or May Not)
Try Men's Souls

Let me tell you some things about strike times. First thing that happened during a strike was that my dad didn't get up at six in the morning and go to work. He got up at six in the morning, got the newspaper, and sat down in the living room in his pajamas to read it. He'd get up, go to the bathroom, light up a cigarette, get the paper, sit down in his big green armchair and start reading. He read the paper from start to finish, beginning with the front page, following every story. He read the comics, laughing and reading the funniest ones out loud to me while I got ready for school. He finished by reading the sports page. He cussed and laughed and carried on about every athlete and every game that ever got played—any sport, any time. After the paper, he'd make some breakfast: eggs scrambled hard, burned toast—no butter—black coffee or a glass of milk (we had powdered milk, made up in a pitcher. Mother said it tasted just the same as the milk from the dairy case. It didn't.) That's my favorite breakfast to this day. Sometimes I wake up with a true and honest craving for burnt toast and those hard eggs with ketchup.

After breakfast, Dad got dressed and went for a walk. I was at school by that time, but he'd go for a walk, usually to buy a pack of cigarettes. See, my mother hated the idea that Dad smoked. She refused to buy them for him, she refused to let him buy them by the carton. It was sort of a matter of principle with her. It was probably a good idea and would have worked as a deterrent with anyone else, but my father loved to take walks, and walking to the little corner market to get a pack of cigarettes was a treat for him, so he wasn't in the least discouraged by Mother's boycott. He'd walk down to the market, Brucie's Groceries, talking to all the little kids playing on the sidewalk, looking at what the neighbors were doing, humming or whistling, just doing the stuff people who take walks do. Then he'd come back home, listen to the radio (or turn on the TV, when we finally got one) and wait for me to get home. Sometimes he'd help Mother hang clothes out to dry or he'd hang around the kitchen and tease her until she threw him out.

The worst part of strike times was the way they worried my mother. She knew for a fact that each and every strike was going to mean the end of every comfort she'd ever known in her life. Groceries were given to us by the union or charged at Martinez's Market. The bills were paid late or not at all. The house payment was late or borrowed from Mother's brother. My mother worried each crisis through to its finish and each crisis was more food for worry than the one before it. Dad's answer to her worries was to laugh and joke and tease so that she'd forget them. Sometimes it worked; sometimes it didn't.

The strikes made her worried, and being worried made her angry as often as not. She saw our various shortages and deprivations as the direct result, not just of a strike, but of my father's lack of ambition. He would never be part of Kaiser Steel's management team, free from union matters. He would not "better himself." No matter how many times the promotion to a management position was offered, the answer was always no. He was "union," and always would be, and the offer of more money and the opportunity to tell his peers what to do didn't appeal to him in the least. If Mother was worried and grouchy, if there were "altercations" (domestic squabbles), if there were hard times, they would pass—it would all pass, but Dad would be exactly what he was, which was "Union—and proud of it."

Now I'm going to tell you some good things about strikes. Did you ever hear of City Chicken? City Chicken is strike times food. Here's the way it went together: Mother bought ground veal, which used to be a real cheap meat, mixed it with an egg and a *whole lot* of bread crumbs (made from the heels of loaves of bread because Dad and I didn't like the heel and always left it in the bread package) and a chopped-up onion. Then she'd mix it all together, shape it into something that sort of looked like the meat part of a chicken drumstick, and stick an ice cream stick into it. She'd roll that around in some flour and bake it and, when it came out of the oven, it looked a little like chicken drumsticks. That was the meat part of the meal. Along with it, we had lima beans cooked with ham hocks. In strike times, we had more lima beans than I care to think about. They were usually cooked in Mother's pressure cooker (the old-fashioned kind that delivered a lot of food to the ceilings of homes across the nation) and smelled just like wallpaper paste to me. We had them for company and for Sunday dinner. We ate them twice a week during strike times: sometimes with City Chicken, sometimes with hot dogs, sometimes with stringy roast beef, sometimes by themselves with cornbread. My mother *believed* in lima beans. (My father loved them, does to this day. I made him a pot just a few months ago and brought them over for him. My mother says she will never cook another damned lima bean if she lives to be 150 years old. She did, however, eat the ones I brought over.)

We also ate nine thousand gallons of chicken soup, chicken and dumplings, beef with vegetable soup, bean soup, potato soup, and pea soup. Being on strike meant scrambled eggs for supper, fried potatoes on the side of everything, soft white bread and bologna sandwiches (no mayonnaise), and no desserts.

It all seemed like a kind of odd holiday to me. Things were different in a very likeable way. There was extra time for things—extra time for me to be with Dad. My father had a very nice voice, for singing or speaking. It was soft and sweet with a lot of smiling in it. When he sang, he sang songs that not very many people knew, and he did a lot of his singing for me, when he was putting me to bed at night during strike times. I'm sure that psychologists now could come up with a bushel basket full of reasons why Dad sang so much when times were hard, but I think it had to do with having the time to sing and a very appreciative audience (me) who knew she could keep her father seated on her bed for at least a half hour, singing and telling the craziest stories in the world if she played her cards right.

Well, first of all, if he was on strike, he didn't have to be up early in the morning, and if he felt like staying up a little later, he could miss a little radio or television time and spend it putting me to bed. He could always, you see, catch the later news broadcasts. Second, Dad felt a little bad about those strikes—no money for extras like movies, or ice cream, or a hamburger from a restaurant on a Sunday drive—not even extra gasoline for the drive. Anyway, he felt a little bit bad about all that and I think he wanted to make up for it. So, he'd tell me to get ready for bed and he'd be in shortly.

He'd come in, sit down on the bed, and say, "What do you want first, Muggsy, a song or a story?" I usually wanted the story first. I'm going to try to re-create one of those stories here for you because I'd be willing to bet a bunch of money that you've never heard any bedtime stories like them. Dad had several wonderful characters who he assured me he knew personally. He knew these people, he said, because he came from Hungary and they were all from the town he was born in or from the surrounding area. There was Ike and Mike who looked alike and had to have a certain famous physician named Dr.

79

Cronkite come cut out their "gazinkeses." (Rhyme the "zink" part of the word with "pink" and you have its pronunciation.) There was the infamous Hungarian Indian, Jerzy Running Bear, who had eight toes on each foot and could climb trees like a monkey. There was Pouter Pigeonni who had a rubber face and could look like anyone in the world and could therefore disguise himself to be *anybody*—Superman, the Lone Ranger, Flash Gordon—*anybody.* The most colorful of all, however, was the brave, handsome, dashing, dumb-but-noble soldier Ivan Awfulitch of the Russian Secret Police Army.

My father told me that as a very young man, he himself had been in the Russian army serving under General Awfulitch. I asked him, "Why were you in the *Russian* army if you were a Hungarian?" "That's just the way it was in the old days," he'd tell me.

See, part of the story was that the same questions and answers had to be exchanged each time. It just wasn't right without them. So, Dad was under the command of the very noble-but-dumb General Ivan Awfulitch. Ivan had been a locomotive engineer before he joined the army. He had no education—could not even read—but he had a fine, long mustache and he was loyal to the Czar and the Czarina, so they made him a General. (Please understand that historical accuracy is meaningless in a really fine fable of the sort my father told.)

Now, here is one of the stories: Once upon a time, Ivan Awfulitch of the Russian Secret Police decided to take his troop of men on a long hike into the mountains of Hungary. It was to be a survival hike to teach the men how to get along in the wilderness. The Czardas Mountain Range was the name of these mountains and they were very treacherous because they were so steep and rocky. The Russian Secret Police Army had very limited supplies, but Ivan was much respected by his fellow Secret Police Officers and was therefore able to get a few supplies to take on this trip. About halfway along the journey, the food began to run out and the men became grouchy and complaining. Ivan was not sure what to do. He made the men sit down and wait while he thought long and hard. He scratched his head, he walked in circles, he sat in the dirt and drew with a stick, he whistled the Russian National Anthem, he smoked a cigar, he kicked his horse, he pulled his ear lobes and finally he got an idea. After the sun went down and the men were all asleep, General Awfulitch got a bag of sugar from his saddlebag. He sprinkled it all over the men. Ah! he thought, when an ant crawls into your shoe or under your shirt, it tickles and tickles until you laugh so hard, the tears run down your face. These men need to laugh. They are too serious. The sugar will bring many ants which will tickle and tickle and the men will laugh. I see now why they made me a general.

The men slept, the ants came. The ants crawled into the men's shirts and into their socks and into their hair and into the remaining food they had with them. Soon the men were all awake and hopping up and down from the itching and tickling of the ants.

"Did all the men laugh, Dad? Did they laugh until the tears ran down their faces?"

"No, They were mad as hell and beat the crap out of the poor old general."

"That's sad, though. He must have felt terrible."

"No, he didn't at all. He thought it was just one more thing he was suffering in honor of the Czar and Czarina, so he was happy."

"What happened then?"

"Well, what do you think? They all had to go back home to their houses in Budapest and eat black bread and potato soup."

"That was OK, then, because they were hungry anyway."

"No, it wasn't OK. When they got back home, they beat up Ivan again."

"Why?"

"Because they hated black bread and potato soup. Their wives and mothers were mostly terrible cooks."

"But that wasn't his fault."

"Doesn't matter. In the Russian Secret Police Army in

the old days they always beat up the generals when things went wrong."

"Did you beat him up too, Dad?"

"No, I never did."

"How come?"

"Because I loved black bread and potato soup. Your grandma made it real good, so I wasn't mad."

"Did Ivan Awfulitch feel bad?"

"Naw. He'd say to himself, 'Wot da hell I care for? Da Czarina she luff me. Da Czar he luff me. All da pipples luff Ivan Awfulitch of da Rooshun Secret Police. Jawohl.'"

And that was the end of one of the stories.

Then it was time for the songs. There were two of them that I liked best. I want to tell you something about having somebody sing to you. If you never have had that, go out right now, find somebody—an aunt or a grandma or a great-uncle—who likes to sing. Not someone who necessarily has a great voice, you understand, because we aren't looking for a professional singer here, but someone who likes music and likes to sing and who knows some odd little songs that not everybody knows. Go out and find that person and invite him over to your house for dinner. After you've eaten and watched whatever you're going to watch on television, or talked over all the things you're going to talk over, get comfortable on the couch or in a big armchair and ask that person to sing you a song. If they demur, press the point a little because, if they like to sing, they'll give in fairly soon and you will be in on one of the nicest things that can happen: being with some- body who's doing something they really love to do and they're doing it for you.

If you grew up being sung to, then you already know how good it is and you can now sit for a few minutes and remember it.

The first song my father sang for me was a funny little song about lavender this and lavender that and kings and queens. The words were only important because he sang them with a smile in his voice and it is that smile that made the foolish song so sweet and so funny.

The second song was a lullaby about "skeeters am

a-hummin' on the honeysuckle vines" and babies in the state of Kentucky. I didn't understand the words for years and years and, when I did, their literal meaning didn't really matter. My father sang that song with such gentleness, such tenderness, that it puts a catch in my voice when I try to tell somebody about it. He sang it like it was the best song he ever knew in his life, like it was some quiet sort of aria from an opera he wrote himself. He sang it like maybe it was the last song he'd ever sing to anybody anytime. And, after he was done, there was never anything left to say—it was just time to go to sleep. Which is what I did.

12

The Photograph
in the Envelope
at the Back of the Album

When there is very little money and even buying groceries looks like it might be a problem, you have to get very innovative about recreation. You have to think of things to do that don't remind you all the time of what you *could* be doing if you only had a little money to do it with. Toward the end of a strike, when things were really getting tough, my mother would say, "I know what we'll do tonight. Let's get out the photo albums and paste some of those loose pictures in it." Then she'd get down about ten big, hard cover picture albums, two or three boxes of loose photos, and a couple of those little flat boxes of gummed corner things—you know, those things that fit right over the corners of the photographs and glue into the album to hold the pictures in place—well, she'd get all that stuff out and put it on the coffee table in the living room. We'd sit around and look at old photos as if we'd never seen them before.

"That's your Uncle Mike—he never could keep his pants up over his stomach.

"Remember that girl? She was Louie's Italian girlfriend—such a pretty girl. I always wondered why he didn't marry her.

"Look, Jack, it's our old Chevy. I had to tie the door shut before we could go anywhere. I'll never forget it. Marti, honey, I used to put you in the car, tie a rope around you and all around the seat and then tie the door shut with another piece of rope before we could drive anyplace.

"Look at Jan there, how thin she is. She always looked about fifteen years old."

"Hey, Marcia, remember that guy? He's the one who lived next door to Sorenson's when he lived in the project. He had the wooden leg and used to like to go to Polish picnics with us when we first moved in there. I think he was sweet on you."

"Oh my God! Look at me in that bathing suit. What's it say on the back of the picture? *Here's me on Christmas Day. Don't you wish you lived in California?* Ha Ha! That was our first Christmas out here, Jack. I looked so thin; I have got to lose ten pounds. Maybe I can do it now that you're on strike."

"Who the hell is that? Some friend of Phil's maybe... no... is that the guy who... no... Oh, I know who it is. It's the guy who was the Helms Bakery truck man for a long time and then he came to work out at the mill and finally got fired for drinking on the job. He went back to being a Helms Bakery truck man after that."

"There's a picture of your grandma, Honey. She's the one you're named after. *Martina*. That's before she got sick—and she'd been one strong woman. My sister Elizabeth's just like her. Both of 'em could throw us boys across the room if they got mad enough."

"Look at this one. Look at that snow... and there's my sister Helen with a snowball and my brother Norby, standing by his first jalopy. He was so proud of that car, took such care of it. You know what? He was good to us, too. He'd say, 'Sis, I'll drive you and Helen over to Ridgeway for the dance tonight if you want to go.' He'd *offer* to take us. He was a real good brother."

"Marti, look at you with that balloon tied in your hair. I made that sunsuit for you. It was just like one that Carmen Miranda wore in a movie—almost the same print and everything. Your crazy father tied the balloon in your hair because he said we didn't have any way to tie bananas and pineapples and grapes onto your head like Carmen Miranda."

"Marcia, here's the one of you and I and Marge and Joe in front of City Hall. This is our wedding picture, Marti. Look how beautiful your mother looks in that suit. Isn't she a sharpie? I didn't look too bad myself. I had that suit made in Cleveland. I used to have *all* my suits tailor-made before I met your mother and she made an honest man out of me. We should put this one in a frame, Honey."

"The color of that suit was called 'Ashes of Roses.' It was my favorite color. I think it still is. Look at how thin Marge looks.

"Look at our old trailer, Jack. It looks so small—how in the world did we ever live in that? Kind of fun, though. I made all the curtains, the bedspread, and most of the furniture. We did a lot of laughing in that dumb trailer. Bob's girlfriend-at-the-time said it looked just like a doll-house inside."

"Your Mama could make anything look good, Marti, even me. She made all my suits for a lot of years."

And on it went through the evening: We'd look at the pictures, put a few in the album and talk about the rest of them. It was fun. But the picture evening I remember best is the one when I found the picture at the back of the album.

It was in a taped-up sealed envelope. It fell out when I picked up the album, so I opened it. It was a studio sort of photograph—posed, with the artificial lighting that professional photographers use—and pretty old. In it were a man and a woman. He was tall (taller than my father), with slicked-back, shiny dark hair and a thin mustache. He looked like a movie star to me (you know the type—fancy-looking, like you'd imagine a Mississippi gambler or a big-time criminal might look). I thought he would be very handsome if he didn't look so serious. I wished he was smiling. He was standing up with his hand on the shoulder of the young woman in an armchair. She was leaning forward a little, so that his hand would rest on her shoulder. She was one of the prettiest, saddest women I'd ever seen in my life. Her hair was down, and it was wavy, parted on the side; it made a kind of little waterfall the way it fell. She was wearing a silky-looking dress with a big lace collar and she was staring into the camera like she was trying to tell it something. She wasn't wearing any jewelry except for a ring on her left hand—it looked like it might be a large diamond. The picture seemed to be of some kind of solemn occasion. I turned the picture over and read: "...and Mary Dombrowski—January, 1939." I couldn't make out the name in front of "Mary Dombrowski."

"But, *you're* 'Mary Dombrowski,'" I said.

My mother and father both looked up. "What?" said Mother.

"*You're* Mary Dombrowski. This isn't you in this picture, Mother. And who's that man? He's handsome...not as handsome as Dad, of course, but he's handsome anyway and that girl has the same name as you and..."

Mother took the picture and looked at it for a long time. There are times when even a kid knows to be quiet. There are times when there's a kind of quiet, like in a funeral home before the funeral starts, and even a kid knows that she better not say anything. "Where did you get this, Marti?" My mother looked like she was mad or worried or something.

"It was in an envelope in the back of the album. I could tell there was a picture in it, so I opened it. Who is it?"

Again, there was that silence. Only, this time, my father and mother started looking at each other. I mean *looking* at each other. I wasn't there, the albums weren't there, the room we were in wasn't even there. There was only my mother and father and the photograph in Mother's hand.

My father finally said, "Maybe you should tell her."

"Tell me what?" I said.

"Marcia," my father said, "maybe you ought to tell Marti."

"Yeah, Mom. Maybe you ought to tell me." Silence. More looking. I can't remember being more curious in my life before or since then about anything. "You gonna tell me, Mom? Who is that lady and that man? How come your name is on the back?" Silence.

"Marsh . . . ?" said my father.

"No," said Mother. She looked at my father and then at me, then at the photograph. "No." She got up, still looking at it, and went into the other room.

My father started stacking up the albums and putting the loose photos back into the boxes. He walked toward the hall to put everything back into the hall closet. "Daddy . . . ?" I wasn't sure what I was going to ask him. He turned around with the albums in his arms and almost smiled at me. "How come—" I started to ask every kind of "how come" question there was, but all of them stopped right before they hit my tongue.

My father stood there for a minute, waiting for me to say something else, I guess, and then he just shook his head and said, "Never mind, Honey." He put everything away and went on down the hall to the bedroom where my mother was. "Goddam strike," he said. "Goddam strike times."

Later, Daddy came out of the bedroom and cooked scrambled eggs for himself and me, but by then it was my bedtime.

I never saw the picture again. I know now what I knew then—that it was my mother and *Someone* in that photograph. *Someone* who had the right to put his hand on my mother's shoulder and pose solemnly for a photographer. Neither of my parents ever offered an explanation and it never seemed right to ask.

* * *

Two weeks after that evening, the strike ended. My father went back to work and there was a huge party in the union hall for the guys and their families. See, that's why I can't help thinking good things about those strike times. I know they always drove poor Mother nuts, but I just can't help it: I think about strike times, and I see my father and Little Billy Marshall and Andy and Bob all grinning behind long tables set up in the union hall, giving out food to all the families of strikers, shouting jokes over the noise of a hundred kids running around loose and crazy in the hall. I took my friend Paulette-from-up-the-street with us one week. We played jacks while Mother waited in line. Then we took our shoes off and started sliding around on the polished wooden floor in our socks, then on our butts, until Paulette picked up a sliver and had to quit. Mother asked Billy's girlfriend if she had tweezers to take the sliver out and Billy overheard it and announced that he'd always thought that strikes were a pain in the ass, now he knew it for sure. Bob Butler suggested immediate amputation of Paulette's butt and Paulette stopped whining and just stared at him until he said, "Well, maybe not this time. But, don't let any of them management guys ever hear you cryin' about a splinter—they'll amputate your butt all the way up to your belly button." Paulette almost started crying again, but Mother said we had got what we came for so we should go. She gave Dad a kiss and Billy and Bob a "look" and we left. At home she gave Paulette the margarine to squish around in the plastic bag until it was all yellow-colored while she took out the splinter. I got to put the pink beans in a bowl and look for little rocks. It was a great day.

The second strike I remember was longer, and it started with what was one of the cardinal sins in Mother's book of *Things You Just Don't Do: r-o-u-g-h-h-o-u-s-e*. There had been a union meeting—a strike was decided on and picket lines chosen. My father was on the line every evening the first week, walking up and down with a sign. He took a flask with him and a thermos of coffee. (Mother only knew about the thermos. The flask was to be "our secret, huh, Muggsy?") On the third or fourth night, it was getting later and later and Dad wasn't home. Mother had called several floozies to see if the other guys were home yet, but she couldn't get hold of anyone because she said that those women like to take camp stools down and watch the "action" at the picket line.

I said, "Can we do that, too? We have camp stools. Can I ask Paulette?"

Mother looked like I had suggested eating stinkbugs for breakfast and said: "No." Just like that.

Anyway, about the time she was going to call the police, a car pulled up in the driveway. It was my father and his merry men. They were chanting as they approached the house—"One step forward, two steps back. One step forward, two steps back"—and laughing like crazy. Mother was watching them through the curtains.

I said, "Is it Dad?"

She said "Yes...and Andy and that damn Butler and —OHMYGOD your father is wearing a *cast!*" By the time she got to "*cast,*" she was hollering and Dad was at the door. The guys had leaned Dad up against the doorframe, rung the doorbell, and run for the car.

Mother opened the door and yelled, "Goddam you, Andy and Bob! I'm going to kill both of you next time I see you. You cowards!"

Dad pulled himself up straight and said, "There's been a little accident, Sweetheart," and gestured toward his cast. My mother started crying right off the bat. "Now, Honey," said my father, "this was really funny. I think you're gonna laugh when you hear this."

My mother stopped crying. She looked a little crazy. "Laugh? Laugh? I don't think so, Jack." She was yelling again. "No. I don't think so! What the hell happened to you?"

My father began to explain how he had been picketing when some scabs tried to cross the line and he had to hit them with his sign and then they tried to cross the line in a car and he and the guys had to stop them so they started to turn the car over by rocking it and that's when he broke his collarbone.

My mother was alternating between hysteria and dumb shock. "Were you drunk?" she hollered.

"Yes, Sweetheart." Dad was being very nice about all the yelling. "I was very drunk. Otherwise I wouldn't have been out there getting the shit knocked out of me. I think I'll go to bed now. Give me a kiss, Muggsy. Good night everybody."

My mother slept with me that night. She said she hoped he'd have the devil's own hangover in the morning and said something in Polish about dog cholera, then we went to sleep. The next day, my father got up at six and made scrambled eggs ("hard, the way we like 'em") for the two of us and read me the funny papers. I got to write "GOOD LUCK IN THE FUTURE" on his cast.

13

Uncles and Aunts
and One or Two
Other Things

Two of my uncles (and aunts
and their families) lived near enough to us to visit when
I was a kid: my Uncle Phil, who was married to my
mother's sister, and my Uncle Gibby, who was my absolute
favorite male in the world, as I told you earlier. He was
about 6'5", very thin, and he had a permanent tan from
riding in his Buick with the top down. (Most beautiful
yellow Buick that was ever made.) He had thinning hair
and a pencil-thin moustache and he got a *manicure* when
he had his hair cut. He lived in a Los Angeles apartment
with my father's sister, Marie, who was (no kidding) about
five feet tall and weighed all of 90 pounds. They both
worked, smoked Benson & Hedges cigarettes, which they
carried in silver cigarette cases, drank like there was no
tomorrow and *had no children*. They were the most sophisticated, suave people I knew and I loved them beyond all
time and space and anything else you can think of.

You probably remember that my Aunt Marie was the

one who was a favorite of her two brothers because of her good sportsmanship and her willingness to join in their misadventures, the one who tried to put out the fire with the teacup. Well, she and my Uncle Gib were really a pair —what you'd call people with a "past."

I want to put some things in here about why those two were what every kid in the world ought to have: They were people who think you're wonderful, people who think your jokes are funny, your IQ is about a million and a half, your hair is just the right color, and you're the prettiest (or handsomest) creature they've ever seen, people who *don't* think that your two cousins are every bit as clever as you are, or who never consider the word "fair" when they bring presents at Christmas—they just bring you the best and biggest and most expensive whatever-it-is because they like you the best. They were what every kid in the world ought to have—and I did.

Many years ago, my very tiny Aunt Marie moved out of her family home in Lorain, Ohio, and found herself a job and a place to live in Cleveland. I believe this occurred in the 1920s. Marie was a bit of a wild child, lots of adventure in her soul. She liked dancing and drinking and meeting new people. The first week she was in Cleveland, she met a sailor who was on leave from his ship. They met in a cabaret, is the way I understand it, and he was one heck of a fine dancer. He was also "cute," in every sense of that word, and Marie fell in love. Within three days, she married him. Within a week, he was back on his ship and, with a smile and a wave, was off to the Orient. The day after he left, Marie called her office and told them she had a cold; she cried all day long. The second day he was gone, she went to work a half-day and cried all afternoon in her apartment. She did, however, manage to get out in the evening for a bite to eat at one of the nearby places she frequented. The third day he was gone, she was at work for the entire day. She went home, showered, changed her clothes, and went out for a drink with a girl-friend. They met two very nice men who took them out for dinner and dancing. She had forgotten to wear her wedding ring, and then felt foolish about explaining her marital status to the gentleman she was dancing with, so she kept quiet about it. The next morning she began crying again, realizing that she'd made a terrible mistake. She had married a man (his last name slipped her mind unless she looked at the marriage license) who had nothing to do with her life whatsoever and, what's more, was probably never going to sail back into it. Not only that, even if he did come back, she didn't want to be married to him. He had seemed very cute after she'd drunk several Pink Squirrels, but the photo she had of him showed a short, somewhat pudgy young man with bowed legs and a squint. Marie cried very, very hard before she finally stopped and decided what had to be done: She called her sister Elizabeth.

"Elizabeth, this is Marie."

"Oh my God, what's the matter?"

"Why do you say that?"

"Why are you calling long distance from Cleveland if there's nothing the matter?"

"I just wanted to talk to you. How's Ma?"

"What's the matter, Marie? Everybody is fine here, now what's the matter with you? You sick?"

"No. Married."

The silence must have been like the silence before an avalanche.

"This better be a joke, Marie. You come home now, *right* now! If it's not a joke, you better be crazy, because I'm going to kill you."

"It's no joke, Elizabeth. I went out with this sailor and we got drunk and went dancing and then I married him and he went back on his boat and left and now I'm married, goddammit, and I don't know what to do and I'm *not* coming home—I'd rather die. This is going to kill Ma, I know it, and Daddy's going to be so mad. Please, Elizabeth, help me just this once. I'll never ask you again, I swear. Just get me out of this."

"What the hell do you want me to do?"

"Get me *un*married. Please, Elizabeth, you know people. You can get me out of this, can't you?"

94

"I'll be there tomorrow. You be ready to do some very fast talking and I'll see what we can do."

Well, as it happened, my Aunt Elizabeth did "know people": judges, court clerks, county clerical workers—my aunt knew lots of people. She came to Cleveland the next afternoon. She hollered, she swore, she threw one or two things (in lieu of throwing Marie, I think), she hollered some more, she shook her finger at Marie. Then she hugged her, told her she was a very dumb girl, and got her "unmarried." I wish I knew the details about how she accomplished that. But, you know, when I heard this story, I was just a kid and they didn't give you all the legal details and stuff. When I asked, "Well, how did they get Aunt Marie *un*married from that guy?" my father would just say, "Oh, your Aunt Elizabeth 'knew people.'" So I knew then that that was one of those things nobody was going to explain to me.

Living in Cleveland in those same days was an extremely handsome man by the name of Albert J. Weisensell, a.k.a. Gibby. How he came to have that name, no one has ever told me. Any time I've ever asked, everybody always shrugged and said, "I don't know. He's been 'Gibby' since I met him." Anyway, he was living alone in Cleveland and working as an accountant for a large jewelry firm, owned by his father. He was technically a married man, but, as my father so profoundly put it, "Fate really kicked poor ol' Gib in the ass." His wife was a permanent resident in an asylum. She had been quite insane since about a year after they married and had not lived outside the mental institution since being committed. Her condition was a deteriorative one and the prognosis was that she'd never be well again.

Gibby and his wife were Roman Catholic, and had been married in the Church. In those days, the Church did not recognize divorce as an alternative to an impossible lifestyle and so Gibby was condemned to live alone forever.

Now, I'm not going to go on and on about this sad situation, because the rest of my aunt and uncle's story is really nifty. So you have all the background you really

95

need. I know a lot more about my Aunt Marie's life before she met Uncle Gib because she was my father's sister
and I got to hear a lot of stories about her. My Uncle Gib
was a bit of a mystery because none of his relatives ever
lived in California so they didn't visit us and tell stories
about him. You know all you really need to know, anyway,
so here's the good part: There was a drugstore near my
aunt's office. She liked it for lunch because she could get a
bowl of soup and a sandwich at their lunch counter for
thirty-five cents. (I don't know if that's the exact price, but
it was some ridiculously small amount of money.) She
went there almost every day and on one of those days, she
sat down on the stool at the end of the counter. Just as she
was about to order, a tall, tall, TALL thin man with a
Rhett Butler moustache walked up to her and said politely, "Would it be all right with you if I sat where you're
sitting?"

"No," said my aunt.

"See, the end stool is a little further away from the
counter and there's a little more leg room for a guy like
me. You could just maybe move down one stool and—"

"Get lost," said my aunt.

"Look, I'm not trying to be fresh or anything. I just
want to sit someplace where I can be comfortable. I
usually sit at this stool, but I'm here a little earlier. I get
my lunch hour at eleven instead of twelve like most people, but today—"

"Did I ask for your life story?" asked my aunt. "I
asked you to get lost."

My uncle smiled. He had this great smile—it looked
like he was grinning at every funny thing that had ever
been said. His blue eyes would squint up and shoot out
flashes of light and his mouth would twist a little sideways
and wiseass-looking. "Say," he said, "you're a pretty sharp
cookie for a short kid. What's your name?"

My aunt didn't like being short much. She didn't like
people to notice she was short even more than not liking being short. "Do I need to call a cop, or are you going
to get out of here and leave me alone?"

He smiled again. "Guess I'll sit down at the other end. Thanks anyway, kid." And that's what he did.

The waitress at the lunch counter was a tall redhead named Virginia. She'd worked there a long time and knew all the regulars. "How are you, Al?" she asked my uncle. "You havin' a ham sandwich today?"

"Like always, Cookie—just like always. Coffee first."

Virginia served him his sandwich and his coffee and leaned up against the counter. "Whatcha doin' tonight, Al?"

"Nothing," said my uncle.

"There's a real good movie at—"

"I have work to do tonight, Virginia," he said. "Thanks anyway."

She walked down to the other end of the counter to fill my aunt's coffee cup. "That Al...I'd sure like to get him alone one night. He's cute stuff."

"Is that so?" said my aunt.

"Married, y'know. Got some kind of invalid wife or something. Wouldn't make no difference to me. I can't get to first base with the guy. He's been coming in here for a year or so, always looks good—suit and all—and I talk to him, but he won't bite. I bought new perfume a month ago thinkin' he might like it—'Blue Waltz,' you know? He didn't even notice. He's an accountant in some big jewelry firm, he says. Works for his father and goes home every night regular as clockwork. I don't know what kind of girl he likes, but it ain't me, I guess. Maybe his wife is real beautiful or somethin'. I know one thing for sure, she's one lucky woman. He's a nice guy—always polite and stuff. Cracks a lot of jokes, too. I like that in a guy, a good sense of humor, you know?"

My aunt finished her sandwich. She picked up her purse, took out her wallet, her lipstick, and a mirror. She fixed her face, adjusted what my uncle later said was "a very silly hat," and got off the stool. (My uncle told me he never did figure out what changed her mind, what she'd been thinking about, sitting at the end of the counter, listening to the waitress chatter. He told me that one of the things he always loved best about her was that he

97

didn't know, half the time, what she was thinking. Just about the time he'd get it figured out, she'd switch tracks and surprise the hell out of him. He loved it, he said. He thought she was clever and mysterious and just feisty enough to make life interesting.)

So she got off the stool and walked down to where he was—"Marie," she said to him.

"Huh?" said my uncle.

"My name's Marie, and I *always* get my lunch hour at twelve on the money."

"My name's Al, Marie"—he put out his hand—"my friends call me Gibby. I'd like it if you'd call me Gibby, too."

"I'm here by twelve-ten, Gibby," she said, and walked quickly out of the drugstore.

"I'll be goddammed," said Uncle Gib.

They met at the lunch counter every day after that for a long time. Gib told me that he had to give the guy at the next desk five bucks to change lunch hours with him so he could eat lunch with Marie. One day he said to her, "I guess you heard I'm married."

"I heard," said my aunt.

"It isn't like you think."

"It doesn't matter."

"See, she doesn't even live with me. She lives in an asylum, you know a—"

"I *know* what an asylum is, Gibby."

"She's been there since right after we got married."

"Is she getting better?"

"She's never going to get better. She'll be there until she dies."

"You going to divorce her?"

"I can't. I'm Catholic."

"Well, anyway, it doesn't matter."

"It matters," said Gib.

"How come it matters?"

"Because...maybe you could be late getting back from lunch, huh? Maybe you could have a headache or something and we could go over there to the park and talk."

98

"What are we going to talk about?"

"You sure don't make anything easier, kid," he said. "Could we just go someplace and talk a while?"

"Let's go to my place," said my aunt.

"How come?"

"Because this sounds like one of those talks where I might cry and I don't want to cry in some damn park. If I'm going to cry, I want to cry in my own room. That all right with you?"

So, that's where they went and she did have something to cry about because that's when he told her all the things of his life that were important for her to know, and that's when he told her he loved her, and that's when they decided to live together without benefit of clergy for the rest of their lives, which is just what they did until his wife finally died in that asylum in 1965.

The year following his wife's death, my Uncle Gibby and my Aunt Marie were married in St. Patrick's Catholic Church in Los Angeles. My husband and I stood up for them. The church was right across the street from a small park. "You want to walk through the park, kid?" my uncle asked his new bride.

"No," said my aunt.

"Why not? It's a great day!"

"Because I'm going to cry some more, and, if I'm going to cry, I want to do it in my own room, not in some damn park. Is that OK with you?"

"You bet, kid," he said. Then he flashed his great smile at her. "Is she somethin' or is she somethin'?" he said to us.

They were both somethin'.

My Uncle Gib was much liked by my father and my father's friends because, even though he was a "professional man," he knew what the lunchpail carriers knew about being a man. Read carefully here: "Being a man" had nothing to do with being some kind of macho shithead who had been in the military or went dove hunting in season, or used to be a professional football player, or pulled the wings off flies for fun. Being a man had to do with knowing who the hell you were and why you worked for a living and where you were going in the next hour or so—not the rest of your life—just the next hour or two. And, I'm telling you, these guys knew the things that were important to know.

Picture a summer Sunday, maybe 90 degrees outside. We didn't have air-conditioning. The patio is cleaned off, ten people are over. Uncle Gib and Marie called in the morning to say they were coming, so Dad figured why not make it a party. He asked Bob and Andy and the "gals" and mother bought beer and soda for highballs and pretzels. I want you to see this: At about 5:15 enough alcohol has been consumed to warrant Serious Discussion. My father starts with "Automation." Everybody hates it. It's going to put us all in the poorhouse, even Uncle Gib, not that they aren't already almost there says mother. A floozy agrees (Mother would rather she'd get off her side). Next: "Space Travel." Never happen, not to me, says Uncle Phil, and everybody laughs. Andy says he wouldn't mind going to the moon if it meant the bill collectors would get off his ass, and Uncle Phil says it wouldn't work—the sons of bitches would follow you. (Dad and I definitely get the Look here.) It wouldn't be too bad if there were some good-looking moon women up there, says Uncle Gibby. That's all you think about, says Aunt Marie (who firmly believes in the truth of her statement, and what's more likes that quality in him). Next: beers all around and "the Union." There you go! Uncle Gibby never belonged to one but likes them anyway on my father's behalf. Uncle Phil just got a promotion to a management position so he is no longer a union man. Bob, Andy, and my father give him a hard time on this account, but he says, Jesus, guys. I'm Catholic, I got five kids to support. The union ain't givin' me enough to live on. I *had* to take that promotion. Bob says nobody *has* to do nothin' they don't *want* to do. There's about a five-second tense moment, then Andy says, What the hell, we're all working guys just trying to get along. None of them going to come out of it alive anyhow. Everybody laughs again. Bob's redhead gets up to use "the little girl's room" and Uncle Gibby watches her walk away. Bob watches Gib watching her, proud that she should be getting appreciative glances. I go to get beers and shots all around. Religion: two Catholics, one Protestant, a couple of abstentions. Uncle Phil says, The best thing about the Church is that they let you drink, smoke, dance, sin like hell (another Look) and make up for it with confession on Saturday before Mass on Sunday. Uncle Gib agrees and gives Andy's blonde one wicked wink, and says to me, Come here, Honey. Want to take a ride to the liquor store with me? Top's down. I say, Yes, please. So happy to be with him. My two cousins want to ride along but he says no kids allowed, and gets away with it because he has no children of his own and isn't expected to "behave" as a father would, doesn't have to be fair to everyone. At any rate, all the big issues are resolved, dinner is nowhere near ready, and, when we get back from the liquor store, hilarity will abound.

Are you there? Can you feel that party? You must have had them like that at your house. Somebody reading this is my age and remembers all of this like I remember it. If you don't remember it *exactly* like that, it doesn't mean either one of us is wrong. It just means that more happened than any of us thought about.

14

Television and the Destruction of the Human Brain As Seen by My Mother

In 1953 my father told me that we were the only people in the entire world who did not own a television set. My Uncle Phillip had one, Andy Kushner had one, Bob Butler had one, even Paulette-from-up-the-street had one. She didn't tell me when they bought it, but I knew right away because she started calling me "Buffalo Marti" (compliments of the "Howdy Doody Show"). She also had started dropping little hints about how late she'd been up the night before. She'd say, "I'm so tired. I didn't have to go to bed until ten o'clock so I could watch...Never mind, I'm not supposed to tell." Subtle, that girl. I think sitting on the driveway with the red ants had finally gotten to her.

So we were televisionless while the rest of the world was being entertained and educated. The unfairness was overwhelming. My father talked and dreamed and cajoled and teased and longed for a television. Mother was immovable. Television, she said, was like alcohol or dope.

People sat in front of it "silent as stones" while the art of conversation died and their brains petrified. She wouldn't be surprised if actual brain cells were destroyed by that thing; a person could be driven crazy. What if you closed your eyes to go to sleep at night and those images or whatever they were kept dancing around in your brain and you couldn't get to sleep. Then what?

"Then you could invite the neighbors into your bed to watch television and eat popcorn—all you'd have to do is close your eyes and the show would start."

"Your father has an answer for *everything*, Marti. He thinks he's very funny."

"Aw, Marsh!" Dad was getting a little desperate. "They got wrestling on now—right from the arena, Marsh. They got tag team wrestling and midget wrestling and Gorgeous George and Baron Leone and—"

"Jack," my mother said, "those are, every one of them, perfect reasons why television ought to be out-lawed. That's violence, Jack, violence. You want Marti to see men throwing each other around an arena? Is that the kind of thing you want a future teacher to be seeing every night before she goes to bed? Wrestling?" Mother's voice rose. "Is that what you want? Her mind distorted by tele-vision and violence? How's she ever going to learn Mathe-matics, or History, or Geography, with wrestling on her mind?"

Dad was beginning to lose track of the conversation. (He had the same look on his face as he did the time my Uncle Norbert told him that it was a well-known fact that some women just plain didn't like sex.)

"Marti's going to be a teacher, Jack. We can't have her mind all mixed up with wrestling and television."

Dad was quiet for a minute. Then he smiled. A light of understanding dawned in his face. "OK, Marsh," he said, "I'll just have to catch wrestling over at Bob's or Andy's. I don't want to flatten the brains of any future teachers around here."

He was giving up. I couldn't believe it. "Daddy"—I was about to get into some very heavy whining—"I want a television. Paulette has a television, Judy has a television,

Sandy has a television, everybody but us. I'm going to stop going to school if we can't get one. I don't want to *be* a stupid teacher."

"Well, forgodsakes—what *do* you want to be then?"

"A wrestler," I said and stomped off to my room.

Dad started laughing. "That kid has the greatest sense of humor," he said. "I think she got it from her old man. At least I gave her something."

Mother sniffed bravely. "Go ahead. Make fun. I'll look after you two in spite of yourselves."

I couldn't see how Dad was going to get around this one. The television got further and further out of reach. Mother got firmer and firmer in her resolve not to have one. Dad and I got hungrier and hungrier for that which "everyone else in the world" had.

Nothing moved my mother! One Saturday night, there was a fierce pounding on the door. Mother opened it and there stood two men—one of them was wearing a grocery sack on his head, crayoned black with eyes cut out; the other one was wearing a cheap Halloween blond wig. Both wore undershirts with names on them. The grocery sack guy had MASKED MARVEL on his, the other guy's said GORGEOUS GEORGE.

"Mary Reisz?" asked the Masked Marvel.

Mother sighed. "Yes, Andy."

The Marvel cleared his throat ominously. "Me and George here have come to put on a demonstration wrestling match for poor old Jack Reisz whose wife won't let him get a television even though he works forty hours a week plus overtime in a stinkin' hot steel mill and never complains."

"Billy," Mother said, "does Irene know you're out running around in a blond wig looking foolish?"

"Who's Billy? Who's Irene?" said Gorgeous George. "Where's Jack Reisz and his poor little daughter, Marti, who's the only kid in her entire school who doesn't have a television?"

"Would you two please come in this house before the paperboy or the neighbors see you?" Mother wasn't sure what to do; they looked so dumb, standing out there. She wasn't sure if they really were going to put on some kind of crazy demonstration match, or if they were just saying all that stuff to get her rattled, or if she ought to laugh or throw them out or what.

"Or what" seemed to be winning hands down when I (in what I think must have been a fit of good manners) said, "Would you and Mr. Kushner like a beer before or after the match, Mr. Marshall?"

Mother began to work her face into a veritable mask of discipline. "That's enough! *Mister* Kushner and *Mister* Marshall—"

I don't know for sure, but I think she might have been able to say something sensible before she threw them out if my father hadn't come out of the bathroom just then. "Well, what have we got here?" he said. He was already laughing.

"These two wrestlers came to put on a demonstration match for us, Dad. It's the Masked Marvel and one of the midgets."

Andy started coughing and choking and laughing like crazy. "One of the midgets! One of the goddammed midgets! Oh God, Jackie. She's really a killer. One of the midgets! Honey, that ain't one of the midgets, that's Gorgeous George. Don't you know Gorgeous George?"

"Sure," I said. "I saw him at my Uncle Phillip's house. He's lots bigger than this, though."

Little Billy Marshall was *not* laughing. "He ain't as big as you think he is. Television puts a lot of inches on a guy. I read that right in the newspaper. Television just makes them guys *look* bigger." His blond, straw curls shook with frustration. "I actually done some wrestling at one time, y'know, Jackie. Back home, I did. Bein' short doesn't mean you can't wrestle. I was pretty damn good, too."

"When the hell was this?" said the Marvel. "I don't remember nothin' about wrestling, Billy. In all the time I've known you I don't remember one thing about you wrestling anybody. You remember anything about Billy wrestling, Jack?"

Dad was watching Billy and laughing again. He started fingering Billy's wig. "Why don't you come in and have a beer, Honey," he said. "And I like the fancy underwear." Now Andy was laughing, too, and I was, too.

"How would you like to have your eyes blacked up for you, Jack, and you, too, Kushner?" asked Billy "How the hell would you like ol' Gorgeous George to just turn your faces a couple dozen colors? How'd you like that?" He was shouting now. It was quiet for a minute—a long minute. My dad quit laughing and looked at Andy and then at Billy. Billy looked at both of them. He was still wearing the wig. (Andy had long since taken the grocery sack off his head. I forgot to tell you that.)

"We have to get cleaned up and leave now." My mother's voice was quiet and came from a very far-off place. "The appliance place closes at nine and I wanted to get over there to price the TVs before they closed. I think they have one on sale and I—"

Eight eyes all turned to Mother. "I'll be goddammed," whispered Andy. "How about that? We did it, Jackie. Me and the midget—we did it!"

And then we were all laughing and yelling and Dad was hugging Mother and little Billy was grinning and saying, "Well, Jesus!" over and over. I ran to wash up and get my sweater. "Can I call Paulette to come with us, Mother?"

"No!" Dad hollered. "'Cause we're going to stop at Domenic's after to celebrate!"

"Celebrate what?" Mother muttered (she was putting on her good shoes). "Celebrate what? The destruction of the human brain?"

15

A Visit

It's very funny how you remember things. It's funny how *I* remember things. For instance, I'll be walking up the driveway of my parents' house, I'll get a whiff of their carob tree, and I'll immediately remember the time my Cousin Bill brought me the cashmere coat from Japan. Or, I'll be cooking dinner in my own kitchen and, just about the time the water starts to boil, I'll remember the red Chevy that used to belong to the Mexican guy who lived on the next block when we lived in the Project (a housing development built by Kaiser Steel to house their employees in the late forties). Or, I'll just be about to fall asleep, a Santa Ana will come up through the canyons into the open window, and I'll remember the days and evenings I crouched on the floor of Laurel Hunter's room at San Jose State College while she did the India ink sketch of me that was going to be her wedding gift for my husband and me. I don't know...remembering is funny that way—you can never be sure what's going to trigger what, or why.

What happened is that the other day I drove by Kaiser Steel in Fontana and that's when I remembered the story I'm going to tell you now: When I was twelve years old, my parents decided that it was time to go back home to Ohio. Most of their relatives and friends still lived there, in the same town, in the same houses. Their children went to the same schools and churches they had attended and they often wrote letters to my mother and father that said we miss you and when are you coming back and Sophie So-and-So died last night in her sleep, she was eighty-three. When my parents got those letters, they talked for long, long hours about the place they used to live, about the storm windows that had to go up in October and about the snowplows that came through the streets right after the snow hit and about putting rock salt on the front walks and front steps and front porches so you didn't slip in the slush when the snow started to melt. They talked about the Polish Club and Warren's Bar out by the mill and the dances at the Pavilion in the park. My father would say, "Let's go back in the fall, Marsh. Marti's never been there and I'd like to show her some things."

And my mother would say, "Not this year, Jack. We're still paying off Martinez's from the strike and we can't afford it."

"Seems like it's never the right time. We're always paying off somebody or something."

"Well," my mother would answer, "if you'd consider going into management like Phillip did, we'd have plenty of money to do the things you want to do."

That would usually be the end of the discussion until next time. Finally, after one of those letters and one of those talks, my mother said, "Yes. Let's go in September."

Everything you've ever read or seen in the movies or heard people say when they talk about the East in the fall is true. The leaves on and off the trees look like they've been painted and they crunch under your feet when you walk. The air moves with a sneaky touch of ice behind it and you can tell by looking at the sky that it's thinking about putting out some profound weather changes. If you have long hair, you wear it down so it can blow around when you walk or you tie it up in a scarf. Hats and gloves start showing up, first on old people and infants, later—just before winter—on young and middle-aged people; jackets and coats have to be worn by everybody after the sun goes down. I was East when I was twelve, and I've never forgotten it.

When the train stopped at the station in Lorain and we got off, forty people were there to meet us. (Well, it *felt* like forty people.) Somebody was holding up a sign that said WELCOME HOME JACK AND MARY! and everybody was shouting and crying and grinning and picking up the little kids who were running all over the platform. It was pretty cool outside—late afternoon—and the air was clear except for what looked like tiny black snowflakes that kept blowing around and landing on our clothes. I asked my Cousin Eddie (a bald, fat guy who smiled all the time, which made his look very accessible, so everybody asked him things) what the stuff in the air was. He said, "That's from the mill, Honey. That's what Lorain Steel blows out its smokestacks." I said it looked like black snow and he laughed, said, "It's obvious you never saw snow before," and went on pounding my father on the back and hugging my mother.

I stood quietly for about three minutes until my Cousin Jackie walked over to me. She was my age— maybe a year or two older—and wore Red Cross shoes. "You from California?" she asked.

"Yeah."

"You ever see Elvis Presley?"

"He's been on TV," I said, "but I wasn't allowed to watch him."

"Why?" She looked at me like I had three heads.

"My mother thinks he's kind of, uh, well...kind of nasty."

"Why?" she said again.

"Because he wiggles his hips and his butt."

"MARTINA!!" My mother had a hundred ears, and I got a warning look.

Cousin Jackie was not about to let go of the conversation. "I seen him when he was on TV," she said. "You couldn't even see his butt. I got one-hundred-twenty-three movie magazines and two-hundred-thirteen comic books in my room. Or doesn't your mother let you read those? [She didn't.] You're staying at my house. You like movie magazines?"

I had flunked out on Elvis, but I wasn't about to blow this whole thing. "I can read what I want," I said bravely, hoping my mother wasn't listening. "I have two-hundred-fifty movie magazines in my room." I sent a prayer up to cover such an incredible lie.

"Man!" She was impressed. "How do you buy 'em? You get an allowance?"

"Yes."

"How much?"

I was catching on to this pretty well. "How much do *you* get?" I asked her.

"Seventy-five cents a week, if I don't forget to make my bed in the morning."

"Oh," I said, "I get a dollar, whether I make the bed or not."

"Lucky! Guy darn! I'm telling my mother that your mother doesn't even make you do your bed and you still get a dollar."

"Well, sometimes I make the bed just because I like to." I was promising every God I'd ever heard of everything I could promise if only my mother wouldn't hear this conversation. "I'm kind of a neatnik, and I like the way the room looks with the bed made. [I had gotten the word "neatnik" from my aunt, who had once said to my mother that it was one thing I'd never be.] But making the bed is up to me." The only thing in our house that was ever up to me was which socks I wanted to wear with which dress, and sometimes even *that* wasn't my decision.

"Lucky!" Jackie said again.

"Who's lucky?" My mother's voice. (Thanks a lot, God.)

"*She* is," said Jackie, "because she doesn't have to—"

"LET'S GET GOING, EVERYBODY!" hollered my Uncle Jay.

The luggage was picked up, we all got into our cars, and we were on our way; my mother never heard the rest of Jackie's answer and I promised God I'd never doubt Him again.

I guess we'd been in Ohio about a week before my father decided that I should see Lorain Steel. It was in South Lorain—baddest part of town—and did nothing (my mother said) but "pour a lot of filth into the air and more filth into the bars at quitting time."

I had not been inside the steel mill in Fontana. My father had suggested it many times, but Mother thought it wasn't really a place for a young lady to visit. She had approved this visit because we were in Mom and Dad's hometown, it was a special occasion, and my Aunt Helen had said that she had once allowed her girls to visit the mill with their father. A lot of exciting things happened in South Lorain when my father was a young man, and a lot of them seemed to take place in and around the Lorain Steel Company. So I really wanted to see the place.

We left early in the morning, maybe seven or so, and stopped at a little place near the mill to have coffee (hot chocolate for me) and a doughnut. It was a diner with about twelve stools and two booths. At least four people were in there who Dad knew and considerable hollering and back pounding took place before we got to eat our doughnuts. When we left, my father took a deep breath. He smiled like he did when he was about to have a real good time. "Muggsy, I want you to smell the air around here and remember it. This is the way a steel town smells. Come on now, a real big breath." I did that. The air smelled warm and dark even though it was cold outside—the temperature and the air seemed to be separate things, as a matter of fact. It was pretty cold. You could pretend you were smoking without a cigarette because your breath came out all smokey, but the air was almost cozy with the smell of the steel mill in it. Well, actually it was a taste rather than a smell. It tasted like burning grass and scalded milk in a cheap aluminum pan and I remember it well enough to tell you about it pretty well. My father kept sniffing the air like a coyote and rubbing his hands together in his gloves and saying, "You're gonna love this, Muggsy. This is really going to be fun. I can't wait for you to see the mill." And that's where we went.

We drove up to a gatehouse outside a huge parking lot. A big sign said: SHOW YOUR ID BADGE TO THE GUARD BEFORE ENTERING THESE PREMISES. ALL TRESPASSERS WILL BE PROSECUTED. I knew neither one of us had an ID badge, and I was starting to wonder what a South Lorain jail looked like, when a man stepped out of the gatehouse and up to the car.

"Can I see your ID...Jesus Christ! Red—Red Reisz! Godalmighty! Red! It must be ten years easy. How the hell are ya? Jesus!" My father got out of the car and there was a whole lot more back pounding, like in the diner. "How ya been, Red? How's California? How's the family? What's your brother doin' these days? Louie, right? Jesus! I'll never forget you two assholes!" Dad was laughing and trying to say a word or two here and there, but the old guy wouldn't have it. He kept asking questions and shouting and pumping Dad's hand up and down. Finally, he looked inside the car and saw me. "Well, I'll be damned! Who's the beautiful lady, Red? What's your name, Honey?"

"That's my girl, Gus," said my father. "That's my very own baby girl. She's a beauty, isn't she?"

"I'm not a baby," I said very quietly. "I'm twelve for heaven's sakes, Daddy."

The man, Gus, laughed. "You sure aren't a baby, Honey. You're a young lady. You and your dad go right on in there and show off yourselves to everybody."

He followed our car over to where we parked and started walking over to the mill with us. "We got almost the same old crew, Red. John Lebotsky died about a year ago, but he'd already retired. Wallace Wilson's still here cleanin' up the place—he's got himself a pretty good bunch of guys, likes bein' a supervisor. Tom and Chester Rezitski are still here, still both work day shift. Tom finally got married about five years ago—married a real sweet fat girl from Akron, but Chet never has gotten married. He says he's never been sure if he was OK since that bull kicked him in the nu—I mean, since the bull kicked him. He didn't want some woman gettin' damaged goods. Jesus is still here. They offered him management three, four years ago, he said no. He's got nine kids for Chrissakes, we'd of all understood, but he said no. We got a few new guys, but not too many. They cut back some on working hours since the last strike— not too much overtime for the guys these days. They don't like that much, but whatcha gonna do? Not too much else to do around here. Say! You sure don't say much, do ya', Honey. She don't say much, Red. That's OK. It's nice for a little girl to be quiet. I like 'em like that. I tell my wife women talk too much. It's nice to see a real polite, quiet little girl. Shows she's been brought up good. Look over there, Red, that's a new building. They just put that up about three years ago. They got showers and towel racks and mirrors and a snack bar in there and some vending machines and tables to sit down and eat or have coffee. The union got that for us. You got a building like that in California, Red?" My father hadn't said much the whole time we were walk- ing toward the mill. He just kept nodding his head and smiling and laughing and once in a while he'd say, "No kidding!" or "I'll be damned!" When we got up to the door of the mill, Gus said, "Well, I got to get back. I'll see you when you come out. Good to see you, Red. We miss you around here. Hell! We still talk about the time you and that crazy brother of yours came to work all tanked up and tore up the joint before security—" My father cleared his throat—loudly. They looked at me. "Well, anyways, I'll see you when you leave," Gus said.

The South Lorain Steel Company was the biggest place I'd ever been. When we walked in the door, I never expected it to open into a cave, but that's what it was. I couldn't even see the ceiling and there were ramps and catwalks and scaffolding every place I looked. The light was red-gold and brown and came from the huge fires that burned behind the doors to the Open Hearth. The light came from gold-white steel that was being poured out of buckets big as buildings and the light came from huge factory lamps hung on huge cables from the ceiling. I must have stood looking around for a half hour before I noticed the noise and the men hurrying around. I heard my father say, "Well, what do you think, Muggs? Hot in here, isn't it?"

"Yeah," I said. "Yeah, it's hot." We started walking.

"Let's go over by the Open Hearth," Dad said. "I want you to see it the way I get to see it every day. But you have to have on the right gear."

Goggles and a hard hat was the right gear. These were lying on a bench over in a dark corner by a water fountain. The signs above it said: DON'T FORGET YOUR SALT TABLETS and WEAR PROTECTIVE GEAR AT ALL TIMES. My father made the goggles tight around my head and then put the hard hat on me. It had straps on the inside that rested on top of my head and, when I looked in the mirror above the bench, it looked like the hard hat fit me just fine.

"Hey! That's my gear!" Some man was hollering at us and walking toward us fast. "That's mine, you sonofa-bitch. And what's that kid—" The man stopped about three feet from us. "Jacky? Jack Reisz? Jesus Christ! Hey! Hey, it's Jack Reisz! It's Red Reisz! Hey, you guys, get your asses over here! It's Red Reisz!"

About nine hundred guys crowded around my dad. I stood there with my goggles and my hard hat, hanging on to Dad's hand and looking at all the other goggles and hard hats with the moustaches and smiles underneath them. Those men were hollering in six different languages—no kidding. My father was having his back thumped and his hand pumped in Mexican, Hungarian, Polish, German, and a couple of languages I wasn't sure of.

I was getting pretty warm in the middle of all those guys, so I let go of Dad's hand and walked over to get a better look at the furnaces. I couldn't get too close; the heat even with the door closed was way too intense. It felt like the hottest day I'd ever felt, five times over, but it was one of the most beautiful things in the world. When the big door started to raise and the sirens went off and the guys started shoveling stuff into the opening like crazy, I wasn't even scared. I thought of the pictures of comets at the planetarium and the Milky Way and of a painting I saw once (in a missal) called *Our Lord Leads the Damned Souls from Hell.* I had backed up as far as I could until I was up against a concrete wall several yards away from the big oven in front of me and it was still hotter than seven hundred dollars. The sirens went off again and the door went down and the guys leaned on their big shovels for a while. It must have happened five or six times while I stood there: the siren, the door, the shoveling, the sparks. I couldn't stop watching. I just stood there, wondering if anybody else's father did anything as exciting as work in a steel mill and if they let girls work in them and, if they *did* let girls work in them, would they let them work as many hours as they wanted and would they let a person stand there as long as she wanted to even if her shift was over and she was supposed to go home.

"You like it, Honey?" My father put his arm around me.

"Yes. I like it," I said.

"Me too," he said. "Sometimes I do like you're doing right now. I just stand here and look at it. Makes me late coming home sometimes because I don't hear the whistle. I just stand and look, like you are. Your mom gets a little bit mad about that; she likes me home on time, but I'll tell you a secret, Baby—sometimes I could sit here the whole night and watch it. That's how come I don't mind working till midnight—I can watch it longer." He was quiet for a few minutes. "You're a gal after my own heart, Muggsy, as my old Irish uncle used to say."

"You don't have an Irish uncle, Dad. You're Hungarian."

"Who told you that? Now, who the hell ever told you *that,* I'd like to know because whoever it was..." And he led me back to the bench where I put back the "right gear," and got a drink of water and read the signs again.

We left. We had to get back to my Aunt Helen's house for dinner and more visiting. We were there in plenty of time to wash up and eat. Mother kept looking at me all through dinner. She kept saying I looked tired, my face was flushed, she hoped I wasn't coming down with something, I would have to go to bed early, she would take my temperature.

"Do you feel all right, Honey?" she asked me.

"Fine, Mom," I said.

"How'd you like the mill, Marti?" my Uncle Joe wanted to know. "It's a pretty big place, isn't it?"

"Doesn't it smell awful? I've always hated the smell from that place. So dirty," said my Aunt Helen.

"It's the same where we are, Helen," said my mother. "Smells so dirty I can hardly stand it. Affects my allergies all year round."

I pushed back my chair. "I liked it," I said. "I like the way it smells. I thought it smelled beautiful." And I started to (forgodsakes) cry like some kind of baby or something.

I didn't have a dumb temperature and I wasn't sick, but I ended up in bed early anyway. I could hear Mother in the living room: "My God, Jack. The mill of all places! A twelve-year-old girl in a *steel mill.* What were you thinking about? What am I going to do with you?"

I fell asleep right after that, but sometime during the night, I woke up. My father was standing by the bed.

"Hi, Dad," I said.

"Did you really like it, Muggsy? The mill. Did you have a good time?"

"Yeah. I thought it was beautiful. Someday I'm going to live right next door to a steel mill, Dad, and I'm going to work there and go there whenever I want to." I tried to

116

think of something that would tell him how wonderful I thought it was, how much I loved it. "And you know what, Dad?"

"Maybe," he said.

"Well," I said, "if I ever have a daughter, I'm going to name her Lorain." He just laughed.

16

Chemicals in Real Brewed Coffee and a Kite Story

Six months out of the year, we had Grandpa—my father's father. He was a very small man, probably only five feet tall or so. He was bald except for a little bit of soft white hair on the sides of his little head right over the ears and he had a tremendous moustache, also white but stiff and bristly and kind of sticking out from his upper lip instead of lying down flat. He wore thick glasses and spoke very little English though he understood everything that was said to and around him. And he smoked giant cigars, which pleased my mother no end. She said not only did they stink up the whole house but they were bad for his health and they made her allergies "act up," but who was she to try and change the bad habits of a seventy-five-year-old man. Dad, Grandpa, and I all heartily agreed with her broad acceptance of Grandpa's cigar smoking (but our agreement didn't seem to please her).

Grandpa did three other wonderful things: He had a

shot of bourbon whiskey every morning before his coffee and breakfast, he poured his coffee into his saucer to drink it, and he walked anywhere he wanted to go. He didn't like riding in the car very much; he wanted to get his baseball cap and his cane and take off to explore the world.

Now, right here, I think you should know that there was a little difference of opinion in our house about how wonderful these things were. My mother thought that drinking in the morning was disgusting. My father said that Grandpa had drunk a shot of bourbon whiskey every morning since he could remember. He said that Grandpa had told him that, "Wheesky is for to get blood warm so the body doesn't have to try to work all day on cold blood." It sounded right to me; the thought of cold blood running through all those little veins and things really didn't sound like a workable arrangement. Besides, I thought it smelled good—it was a little like after-shave lotion with a sort of "foody" side smell. I liked it, and I figured that I had the only Grandpa in the world who knew this secret of sending warm blood through his body before he tried to do anything.

The coffee ritual was practically a religious rite. First of all, Grandpa refused to drink the instant coffee which my mother thought was an invention from God. However, he had to have coffee. He told Dad (in Hungarian, with Dad translating which seemed like a bad idea because then Dad took the blame for whatever was said and had to do the arguing for both himself and Grandpa, who just got to sit in the big armchair and look old and wise) that real brewed coffee had a chemical in it that was very good for old people and helped them live a long time. Grandpa said that a doctor friend of his in Hungary had told him that and that man had lived to be 102, so it had to be true, in which case could Marcia please make him real brewed coffee like his beloved Martina (his wife—I'm named after her) always did until the day she died and like my Aunt Marie did when he was at her house in Los Angeles (the other six months of the year). So Mother did it, but she sure didn't like it. He'd get his coffee in the blue cup and saucer he liked and he'd slowly pour the coffee into the saucer, blow on it, and then sort of suck it through his moustache with a great deal of pleasure and noise. I thought it was one of the most skilled maneuvers I'd ever seen; he never spilled a drop and he could drink that whole steaming cup of coffee in a few seconds. I'd get up from the table and get the coffeepot right away to pour some more so he'd do it again. If I was fast enough, he'd do three or four saucers. It was terrific because it made such a great noise and cleaned the toast crumbs out of his moustache.

Poor Mother! She hated whiskey-drinking old folks and saucered coffee as much as she hated dirt and ants. Mother's idea of what old people should be was sort of like a Norman Rockwell painting: you know, old folks with rosy cheeks and round, fat stomachs, giving out little candies and change to children and patting dogs and puttering around the garden until it got too warm and then coming in for a nice glass of iced tea and half of a tuna sandwich with lettuce, then taking a nice nap with the shade down, then getting up in time to take a shower and shave and tell the grandchild/children a couple of stories and then eat a good dinner, read a paper, write a letter or two, listen to the radio, read a little Dickens, and go to bed. My mother firmly believed that that's how *all* old people should be. She was going to be like that when she got old and so should everyone else. If you noticed, there is nothing—not a word—in the above description that covers a shot of bourbon whiskey in the morning and/or saucering and straining coffee through a moustache. There you have it. Grandpa just did not fit the picture.

They had a really bad argument one time because Mother told him that she was "very sorry, Dad, but there is no whiskey in the house and I'm not going out at nine A.M. to get some." Grandpa got up from his chair, walked right to her "hiding cupboard," and said, with a very sweet smile, "See, here it is, Marcia." She was furious and told him never to call her a liar again. He looked like he didn't understand, finished his shot, and started on breakfast.

Another time, when he was about to saucer his coffee, Mother said, "Why don't you just drink it out of the cup, Dad, like other people do?"

"OK, Marcia," he said pleasantly and started to drink from the cup.

"And, Dad, don't slurp it through your moustache this time."

Grandpa waited for what seemed like a long time. Finally he said, "OK, Marcia," and put the cup to his mouth.

I don't know how it happened, but Mother yelled, "Oh for God's sake, Dad," and jumped up from her chair. Grandpa had missed his mouth and the coffee was pouring down his shirt front. I don't know how he could have done it. He never missed his mouth when he was drinking from the saucer. He could soak his toast in it, get the toast into his mouth without losing a drop. But this time, he missed his mouth.

"Oh," he said. "Marcia—a little accident. I am sorry."

"You probably did it on purpose," Mother said.

Grandpa looked at me. "Marti, my darling, I don't understand."

"Marti," said my mother, "go make your bed." I already had. "Then go clean your room and do your homework." I already had. "Then do it *again—now!*" She meant business, I could tell.

Later that night, Grandpa told my father a story in Hungarian. It took a long time to tell and they both laughed a long time after he was done telling it.

Poor Mother, Grandpa was just not the old person she would have chosen to live in her house six months out of the year. He liked old clothes, would put anything new into his bottom dresser drawer and never take it out of the cellophane; his pants were mostly always too big and wrinkled and he wore the same shirt a lot of days in a row. He thought showers were for weddings and funerals and naps were to be taken in armchairs whenever he wanted to take one. He hated candy—liked cigars instead—so he didn't have candy in his pockets and he wordlessly gave me $1's and $5's instead of change. He couldn't speak or read English so it limited the amount of Dickens he could read and he was so small that if he'd tried to take me on his knees and tell me a story, it probably would have fractured his little kneecaps. But, God! He was wonderful. It looked to me like he did everything everybody else was afraid to do: He ate and drank just what he liked, went to sleep when he felt like it, got up when he felt like it, left things right where they were on the floor or on the bathroom sink, didn't make his bed, let cigar ashes drift from his shirt to his pants and to the floor without giving them a second thought. I'm afraid that all those things are exactly the things my mother saw as extremely important and so she and Grandpa were not the best of friends as friends go.

I almost forgot to tell you about that third thing Grandpa did: He walked. *Everywhere.* He'd put on his dark blue baseball cap, get his cane, and start walking. He had done it all his life. In the old neighborhood (Lorain, Ohio) all the stores were in walking distance and everybody knew everybody and walking was a kind of adventure because he'd see people he knew at the stores and the barber shop and the newstand and they could stand around, smoke, tell jokes, and maybe go for a drink later —before dinner. Walking was a real vocation, a thing he *did.*

Well, when Grandpa moved out to Southern California to be with us, he figured he would do the same things he had always done. He would walk the neighborhood, meet everyone worth meeting, find out where the best talking places were and go there. Things were different there, though. My father tried to explain to Grandpa that most people drove around in California and that people didn't stop at corner grocery stores to chat (he left out "especially with old people"). But Grandpa didn't buy that. He supposed people were the same everywhere— even in California—and he wanted his walks. My father insisted, my grandfather insisted back (all in Hungarian), my mother stood toe-to-toe with each of them saying, "Jack, tell him..." and "Explain to him, Jack..." It looked to me like Grandpa was winning. He was doing the least amount of talking and, behind his glasses, back behind his eyes, I was sure I could see the gleam of victory. Finally, he sat down in the armchair with his cane still in his hand and his baseball cap on and said very, very quietly in English, "OK, Jackie. OK." I'm not certain my parents heard him—they were, by this time, arguing with each other. Grandpa was getting out a cigar. And so it came to pass that Grandpa didn't take his walks anymore ...when my father and mother were home. He would wait until I got home from school, that's when mother would run errands, or do the things she liked to do. I'd be home and could "watch Grandpa," so he didn't burn the house down while she was gone.

As soon as she was out of the driveway and had turned the corner at the end of the street, Grandpa would go get his cap and his cane, kiss my cheek, smile, and say, "I go a little while, Marti, my darling. You stay."

I'd say, "Hurry back, Grandpa. One hour—OK?"

"OK, my Martina. One hour. OK." And he kept his word. He'd be back in one hour. It didn't seem like a bad thing to do. He was an adult person. I didn't figure it was my place to tell an adult person not to take a walk if they wanted to, no matter what Mother said. (I still feel that way.)

I'm going to tell you how something went wrong with the walking one time. But, to do that, I have to tell you how something went wrong with a kite.

I love kites—always have, still do. I got a new one every year and Dad would put it together for me and go out in the field down the street from us and fly it with me.

One year, I got a new kite, Dad put it together for me, but had to walk a picket line in the afternoon and couldn't fly it with me that day. "Tomorrow, Muggsy," he said. Mother drove him out to the mill to picket and she went to the union hall to pick up our surplus food items.

Grandpa and I were alone. I decided that I could certainly fly a kite alone and would go out to the field for a while and do just that. The wind was right and the kite went up like a dream. I flew it for an hour, then another hour; I flew it until I realized that I had let all the string out almost and had sort of ambled out into the field and across to a neighboring field.

I started reeling in the kite and by-and-by it was cold and by-and-by it was late and getting dark and still my kite was out there on the end of a string, which must have been two miles long. I couldn't just cut the string and let it go. The kite and string had cost nearly one dollar. My father had bought it for me even though we were on strike; a dollar was a lot of money. I couldn't let go of such a beautiful kite. I could feel that kite up there, pulling on the string, and so I kept reeling it in.

It was pretty dark when I heard my father yelling my name. "I'm over here, Dad," I yelled. "I can't get my kite in."

He came running like crazy. "Where the hell have you been? We thought you were lost. Your mother is hysterical. She's looking in all the neighbors' trash cans for your dead body. The police are looking for you. Andy and Bob are out looking for you. You scared us to death, Honey!"

I explained how the kite cost so much money, that it was my favorite color of green, that it was the best flying kite I'd ever had, and how I couldn't just let go of it as long as I knew it was still up there. My father was quiet for a long time. He just stood there, looking at me. Then he hugged me, said I was going to make some guy very happy someday (which I did not understand at all then), and cut the string.

We went home, Andy and Bob came, and Mother stopped crying. Everybody was about to have a short snort and a beer when Dad said, "Muggsy, go get Grandpa out of his room. I bet he'd like a belt."

I went and came back real fast. "Daddy," I said, "Grandpa isn't in his room."

"*Shit!*" yelled my father. "*Shit, shit, shit!*" Andy put on his jacket, Bob buttoned his sweater, Mother started crying again and called the police. Everybody but me and Mother went searching for Grandpa.

About eleven P.M., the police brought him home. He was cold, a little confused, but otherwise fine. It seems that when all the excitement started, he saw the chance to go for a really long walk, which he did. He explored places we'll never know about, I'm sure. But, when it started to get dark, he stopped in a little bar to warm up before he walked home. After a couple of drinks, he'd decided to make the most of a good thing and just keep walking until he felt like stopping.

"Where did you find him?" my father asked the policeman.

"We didn't, Mr. Reisz. He found us. He walked right up to the car, gave us a piece of paper with your name and address and phone number on it, and said 'Home, please.' So we brought him home."

Mother was still crying. "God—oh God! Is he all right? Maybe we ought to take him to the hospital."

"I think he's just fine, Mrs. Reisz. He was laughing and humming all the way here in the car. I think he's feeling just fine."

My mother was not happy. "Well, I'm glad *he's* fine," she hollered. "The rest of us will be recovering from nervous breakdowns the rest of the week."

Dad went over to Grandpa. "How are you feeling, Daddy?" he asked.

"Good, Jackie," said my grandfather in English. "Good walk. Very good drink. Good ride. I go to bed now."

He started toward his room and then turned and said something to my father in Hungarian. My father laughed as hard as I'd ever heard him. Andy and Bob and Mother and I all looked at him, waiting to hear what Grandpa had said. Grandpa went down the hall and into his room. Dad was still laughing.

"What'd he say, Jack? What's so funny?" Now he was laughing so hard he was crying. "I don't see one funny thing in all of this, Jack Reisz." My mother was getting mad.

"Oh God, Marsh," said Daddy. "He said he'd had a fine evening, that there was a very nice lady in the bar who said he was very sweet. He bought her a drink, and when he got tired, she didn't want him to leave. He wants to go back tomorrow night."

Bob and Andy and I started laughing, too. "Well, hell, I would, too," Bob said, "if some pretty woman told me I was sweet when I was seventy-some years old! Will you think I'm sweet when I'm seventy, Mary? Come on, Mary. You will, won't ya? You'll still be crazy about me, right?"

"Bob Butler, I can hardly put up with you now. I don't even want to *know* you when you're seventy. I'm glad you all find this so funny. I'm going to bed. Marti—bed!"

They were up until all hours that night. My father was telling stories about my grandfather as a young man. Every once in a while, I'd hear Andy said, "He wants to go back. Don't that beat all? Jesus, Jack! What a sport!"

It was always going to be a good story. I could tell, because Dad said, "Wait'll I tell the guys at Domenic's. They're gonna shit!"

17

A Birthday
and a Polish Party

My mother did not like to entertain. The idea of throwing a "party" gave her hives and made her very grumpy, so it wasn't a thing we did very often. However, the year my father turned fifty was a major occasion and my mother felt that it ought to be celebrated in style with a real party—a surprise party, at that. A good surprise party is difficult even for the most practiced party giver and I think it would be safe to say that the host or hostess has to be able to depend on the person he or she asks to get the victim to the party site at just the right time. The guests have to be there already, quiet and ready to holler "*Surprise!*" The food has to be ready. It all has to be together before the honored guest arrives with those who have kept him/her away from the house until all is in readiness. It is that element of dependability that makes all the difference, and it was that element of dependability that was the downfall of my mother's surprise birthday party for Dad.

She did it all with finesse. The menu was planned: a buffet dinner. The guests were invited: twelve of them. The co-conspirators were chosen: Andy, Bob, and my Uncle Gib. It was decided that Andy, Bob, and Uncle Gib would suggest taking Dad out for a drink; his birthday happened to fall that year on a Saturday. Uncle Gib and Aunt Marie would drop over in the afternoon, then Andy would call and suggest a quick birthday drink with Dad and Bob, and Mother would say, "Go ahead, Honey—you and Gib go for a while. Marie and I'll make hamburgers to barbecue later." Then the guys would bring Dad home about 7:30 when everything had been prepared and everyone else had arrived.

At first everything went according to plan. About 5:00, Andy called. Dad and Uncle Gib left. Mother and Uncle Gib exchanged knowing glances. All was well.

About 8:00, Mother began looking at her watch. The table was covered with all kinds of great food—all of Dad's favorites—and everybody had a drink in hand. Conversation seemed easy and Mother wasn't really worried, just aware of the time and of the food cooling rapidly on the table. At 8:30 Mother called Andy's, then Bob's—no answer. She smiled a little nervously, poured everyone another drink and put a couple of the casserole dishes back in the oven to stay warm. At 9:00 Mother called Andy's, then Bob's—no answer. She managed a somewhat shaky smile for her guests and went into the kitchen to check the food. She started looking out the front window, looking up and down the street. At 9:30 Mother called Andy's, then Bob's—no answer. Mother stopped smiling altogether, poured everyone another drink and started muttering something about did they still give the gas chamber for murder even if it was for a good reason.

At 9:50 my Uncle Gib's Buick pulled up in the driveway. Out of that Buick crawled the four drunkest men I had ever seen in my life. They were singing "The Golden Earring," a Hungarian song that my father and my Aunt Marie often sang together after a few beers. This time it was Andy and Bob and Dad and my uncle singing it in what passed in their minds for harmony.

Ah, but picture it! It was 9:50. The food was cold. The guests were hungry, sleepy, and a little polluted. My mother was angry and embarrassed and not sure what to do about it as long as company was there. Up the driveway they came singing, arms around each other, they opened the door and a few weak voices shouted "Surprise!"

My father said, "Well, I'll be damned! Isn't this just the nicest thing? Isn't it? You knew about this, Gib? You, Andy? You, Bob? I'll be damned." He kissed Mother and me and shook hands all around and everybody kind of woke up and started laughing and making jokes.

That's when Mother noticed he was walking funny, sort of hobbling around. "What's wrong with your leg, Jack?" She didn't ask it in a very friendly way. She looked down a little closer and said, "Oh my God! Oh no!" My father was wearing a huge black bowling ball attached to his ankle by some chain and a handcuff.

"We can't find the key, Marcia, Honey. We can't. Nobody's got it. Not Gib, not Bob, not ol' Andy—nobody, Marcia." And Daddy started laughing his head off.

My mother wasn't laughing—not even a little.

"Hey, Marcia," said my Uncle Gib, "I wish you gals could've been there. Old Jack is sitting in Domenic's and we get Dom's wife to make him over a little bit, you know, kind of mess up his hair and keep him busy thinking of other things. . . . She did, too, Marcia, you should've seen her. She gave Jack a birthday kiss and brought him a free shot of Kessler's—"

Mother was *not* smiling. It didn't look to me like she thought Domenic's wife had done a very good thing at all.

"—then Bob here dropped his lighter and cigs down by Jack's leg and we slapped that cuff on quicker than anything you ever saw while Jack was busy loving up— what's Dom's wife's name, Jack?—oh yeah, Carly. Goddam, Marcia! It was great! Jack never knew what hit him. The only thing is that I can't find the damn key. I thought

I had it in the glove compartment... Isn't that where we put it, Marie?"

My Aunt Marie was laughing so hard she had to sit down. She just kept shaking her head and laughing and not telling anyone where she thought the key might be. Everybody was pretty much laughing—the drinks and no food yet had something to do with that, I think.

There was Dad with that dumb thing on his leg, drunk as hell; he was standing in the living room with one arm around me and one arm around Andy, and he was saying hello and how are you to everybody. His hair was all messed up, and he smelled great—like beer and cigarettes and Kessler's "Smooth As Silk" Whiskey. The guys were all shouting and carrying on and laughing like they always did and I was thinking that I wanted every birthday party I ever had in my life to be just like this one.

My mother said, "For heaven's sake, let's eat. Can you eat with that thing on your leg, Jack?"

"Hell yes, Honey," my father said. "I don't eat with my leg, do I?" And everybody started in laughing again and went for the cooled-off food in the kitchen like they hadn't eaten in a month.

Dad hobbled in and started shouting about how every single one of his favorite foods was on that table and how Mother was a goddam genius in the kitchen and how did she do it all without him knowing. She kind of forgot then about Carly and how late things got started and she put her arms around Dad and said, "Happy Birthday, Sweetheart. It was easy to do this party—nothing at all, really. Marti, eat at least one of those cabbage rolls and don't take off the cabbage and throw it away like you usually do. Jan, I made the meatballs like you do, with no tomato sauce—Jack loves them that way. Those dumplings were just too big to fit in one bowl, but there's plenty more of them and more of the paprikash, too, so have all you want!" She was happy. The rest of the evening she was running around making sure the bowls stayed full of food. My Uncle Phillip fixed drinks for everybody all night and Bob Butler gave me a glass of Vernor's ginger ale with just a "taste" of Kessler's in it so

I'd "sleep all right with all this noise going on." Mother only got a little bit mad when Clyde Hall from next door was hacksawing the cuff off of Daddy's leg (they weren't kidding, they couldn't find the key) and when she heard my Uncle Gib ask Billy Marshall's girlfriend if Dom's wife always gave everybody that kind of birthday kiss, because, if she did, he was going to make sure that he spent every birthday for the rest of his life over at Domenic's.

This is a good place to tell about another kind of party. While we didn't give a lot of parties, we went to quite a few because we had lots of relatives and that meant weddings and funerals and birthdays, etc., and those kinds of gatherings are always good for a story that is remembered for a long time.

I'm not sure if I mentioned it or not: my mother is of Polish extraction. Her mother and father and oldest sister were born in Poland. Those roots became important in my life for several reasons. First, Polish food is good! The pastry is all butter and yeast dough and deep-fried stuff. The beef and pork is usually ground up and wrapped in cooked cabbage or made into little turnovers, and the chicken is cooked in water and spices until the whole world smells like chicken and then it's served with home-made noodles or dumplings. Second, Polish parties are the rowdiest, craziest parties that ever happened. Really. When I was eight or nine, we went to a Polish wedding that was so wild it'd take the skin off your teeth (that's the phrase Dad always used). I'll tell you about it because it was so much fun and because it's a good story about my mother, who is not going to like it when I put it in here.

Once, we went to Ohio because my cousin, Jacqueline, was getting married. She got married in a Polish-language Catholic Church at eleven A.M. The reception began at two at the Polish Club—a popular bar and restaurant that rented its premises to people for their parties. The reception started off like always. The band was a four-piece:—drums, accordion, saxophone, and piano—and they played a wide range of polkas and ballads (those are the only two kinds of music that go over at Polish wedding receptions). There was plenty of food and plenty of beer and wine and plenty of bourbon to go along with the beer. My mother, who rarely drank anything alcoholic, allowed herself to be brought beer after beer while she polkaed and waltzed with all the men she knew there.

About 1:30 in the morning, my father grabbed my mother off the dance floor where she was doing one hell of an energetic polka with my Great-Uncle Tony. At 5'7", he weighed 280 pounds and was well-known in Lorain as the best polka dancer in Ohio. Women waited in line at the Polish Club to dance with my Great-Uncle Tony. He was half "Eyetalian" and half Polish. Everybody said that was why he could not only dance well, but for a long time. Then Dad grabbed me out of the arms of my Great-Uncle Stanley (who was very old and a good sport about dancing with children) and said to my mother, "I think we better go, Marcia. Your brother Joe just called some guy a 'goddam spic' and invited the guy to hit him in the stomach. Your brother Norby is trying to stop the whole thing, but I think there's going to be a fight and I don't want my girls in the middle of it."

My mother was very protective of her brothers and she'd had about eleven or twelve beers and a couple of shots, so she was feeling pretty feisty. "I'm not going anywhere!" she said. "Who's picking on my Joe? I'll teach him a few things—where is he?" And off she went to protect her brother who was prince of the Polish hell-raisers and perfectly capable of getting himself in and out of his own troubles.

My father started to get a little bit up for the whole thing, too. "Marcia," he said running after her, "I'll take care of this. You take care of Marti."

Mother handed me back to Great-Uncle Stanley. "Stash," she hollered, "watch Marti until we get back." She followed my father to a corner of the club where there was some pretty loud shouting going on by this time.

My Great-Uncle Stanley took me to a table and said, "We'll wait here until everybody's ready to go home." I guess I fell asleep right there at the table because, when I woke up, I was in my Uncle Jay's car; he was driving and my father was talking to him, "I never saw anything like that in my life, Jay. You were dancing and missed the whole thing. Marcia went running over to where Joe and Norby were standing arguing with this little guy from Amherst. Joe was saying that he never knew the guy's sister eight years ago, or ever, and that he had the wrong guy. The little guy was saying that his sister told him that Joe Dombrowski was the guy who tried to get fresh with her at the Sacred Heart Valentine's Day dance eight years ago and called her a bad name when she wouldn't let him get away with it. Joe said he never knew her and besides, he didn't go out with Puerto Rican girls. Then the little guy says, 'Why, what's a matter with Puerto Rican girls?' and Joe says, 'Well, you never know where they been.' That made the little guy real pissed off and he called Joe a 'stupid Polack pig' and took a swing at him. Marsh got so goddam mad! I've never seen her that mad. She went after that little guy like crazy. Norby tried to stop her, I tried, Joe tried, but the next thing I knew, she was up on the bandstand and"—he turned to my mother—"I didn't even think you could pick up that goddam accordion much less *hit* somebody with it, Marcia. Jesus Christ! That was one surprised Puerto Rican. Dr. Lupinski said he didn't think it would take more than three or four stitches to take care of the guy's head, but, hell, I don't know, it looked worse than that to me."

"Mother *hit* somebody?" I said, really awake now.

"No, of course not, Marti. Your father's kidding again. Go back to sleep."

"With an accordion, Mother? Really you did?" I couldn't believe what I'd heard.

"I said I didn't hit anybody. Go to sleep, we'll be at Aunt Helen's in a little while."

I was about to go back to sleep when I heard Dad say, "You should've seen it, Jay. Boy! If I'm ever in a bad spot I'll just call on the little woman here. She damn near killed that guy. You should've seen it. He'll think twice before he calls anybody a 'stupid Polack pig' again. Old

Joe just stood there with his mouth open watching Marsh go after that guy."

"Jack," my mother said, "if Marti hears and remembers any of this, I'm going to kill you. Now just be quiet and let's forget the whole thing."

I sat there with my head against the seat pretending to be dead to the world. I figured I'd better do whatever she said; I didn't want anyone who almost killed a Puerto Rican with an accordion to go after my father.

18

My Father
and Ann Sheridan;
My Mother
and Cary Grant

We were church-going peo-
ple. My mother was a woman who believed that everything should be backed up with tangible proof. If you
were a believer of any sort, you ought to be a church-goer
so that when you were out with people and they said,
"What religion are you?" you could then say, "We're Presbyterian [Methodist, Baptist, Episcopalian, Foursquare,
etc.]." Or, if you were out somewhere doing something
you really didn't want to do with people you really didn't
want to do it with on a Saturday night, you could say,
"Well, church tomorrow. We'd better get going, it's almost
nine." *Nice* people, my mother said, didn't argue with that
and were gracious about letting you go home. My father
said, "Yeah—nice people and people who don't care if
you go home because they don't like you too much in the
first place." My father never knew when not to say things
like that.

We were Presbyterians. My mother had, early in her

life, rejected her Roman Catholic upbringing. She was the only one in her entire family, in fact, who was not a practicing Catholic. Her reasons were never made clear to me. She told me that "Each person should find God in their own way and it's not up to anyone to have to explain what that way is, as long as it isn't a heathen religion like Buddhism or Voodoo or something." It was the only explanation I ever got. I don't know any other reason to this day.

Anyway, we went to the First Presbyterian Church in a small town about ten miles from us. It was a large white building and the people who attended services there were people with "a little sophistication," said Mother. (I strongly suspect that "a little sophistication" is like "a little knowledge" about brain surgery—somewhat foolhardy and very dangerous.) You could tell they were sophisticated because the men wore hats and the women wore hats and gloves and they smiled very small, tight smiles that pinched their cheeks up. They all shook hands with the minister after the service, told him they liked the sermon, and then stood around outside to greet each other. My father said that they were really standing around to see who was there who hadn't been on the last Sunday or two so they could ask them, "Where have you been? We've missed you." Then they could hear if any grief or scandal was going on that could be talked about at a later date. My mother said they were simply "good Christian people who were interested in their Christian brothers and sisters." My father said where was their interest during the last strike when we were about down to our last cent and the chairman of the Tithing Committee called to ask why we hadn't tithed lately. Mother said everyone had troubles of their own. Even the Presbyterian Church—"And you can just get dressed because we're going whether you want to or not, Jack." My father whispered to me that it seemed to him that there was something very wrong with going to church whether he wanted to or not. I whispered, "Me too." It was just about the last thing I ever whispered in my life. (You know, I think my mother inherited her ears from a rabbit and her eyesight from an owl. She could hear stuff that you said down the hall in the bathroom with the shower running and the toilet flushing. And she could see what you were doing in your own bedroom when she was at Martinez's Market six miles away.) Anyway, she heard me whisper "Me too" and came down the hallway with fire in her eyes.

"You too, huh? Well, you can just tell that to Jesus when you get to church this morning, Miss. You can just tell him 'I didn't want to come here and visit you this morning, Jesus. My mother wanted to come, but my father and I didn't. We know you do everything for us and that you love us, but we just didn't want to visit with you at your house this morning. Maybe next week would be better, Jesus.' I want you to say that this morning, Miss Marti."

I must have been all of seven years old or something like that and I was not at all certain how Jesus would react to that kind of declaration. He looked like a nice man in all his pictures, but I hadn't ever met him personally and, since my father said, "You can't figure out what a guy's like until you know him yourself; you can't go by what other people tell you about him," I decided not to say too much to Jesus about visiting him and all that until we knew each other a little better. Besides, Paulette's Aunt Fran and Uncle Gaylord went to church one Sunday and they went down to the altar to talk to Jesus about Uncle Gaylord's gambling and drinking and, when they were standing there telling Jesus about it, a bolt of lightning came out of their minister's hand and knocked Uncle Gaylord *and* Aunt Fran right on their backsides. Aunt Fran didn't even have any bad sins to talk to Jesus about and He still knocked her on her butt and, get this, neither her or Uncle Gaylord could say a single word for one week! They had been struck *dumb* by Jesus! Paulette told me that, and her mother said it was true. So, if Jesus would do that, no telling what He'd do if you said outright that you didn't feel like visiting Him that morning. Thinking about it made me worry a little about my father, who kind of had to be talked into church *every* Sunday, but Dad got along with everyone he ever met—everybody liked him—so, I figured he probably had made enough of a hit with Jesus to be safe.

By this time, Dad was putting on his tie and I knew he was going to go to church and to the adult Sunday School class afterward to make Mother happy. That meant I would have to go to Sunday School after the regular service, too—not one of my favorite activities. Mother was putting her hat on. She looked beautiful; it was one of those small hats with a net that came over her eyes and made her look mysterious. She was looking in the mirror and had the smart-alecky look on her face that she got when she knew she looked good. "Jack"—she smiled at herself—"I want to invite someone to come over after church today. The Bensons or the Palmers—they're nice people. The Bensons could bring Laura and Marti would have someone to play with."

My father looked at me. I shook my head no with all the intensity I could muster without Mother feeling the breeze. "Ah, Marsh," Dad said, "I don't want to do that. I thought I might take you gals out for a hamburger after church today and then maybe we could take a ride someplace."

"I *like* the Bensons," my mother said. "They don't drink or smoke or swear. Lucy Benson has read *everything*, and Marti loves to visit Laura."

CORRECTIONCORRECTIONCORRECTION

You need to know something here. I was a kid who read. I didn't have brothers or sisters or too many friends so I began to read very early in my life. I read just about everything I could get my hands on. You know, the kind of person who reads books, magazines, newspapers, cereal boxes—everything (except comic books and movie magazines, which my mother said were trash and I was not allowed to have them in the house or buy them. Paulette let me read hers for twenty-five cents, which was exactly half my allowance for the week. I quit doing that when Judith from across the street baby-sat for me and let me read hers for nothing).

I was one reading son of a gun, and the only thing I liked about weird Laura Benson was the fact that she had a room of her own that had been built for her in back of their main house, and it was full of bookshelves and books. Mrs. Benson was a librarian and was able to buy books from the library—old books that would have been discarded because they were being replaced—for practically no money at all. So, Laura Benson had every book there was. When we visited, all I did was curl up in a corner of her room and read until it was time to go home. Mother saw that as an indication that I was, despite her worst fears, a social animal who knew a class act in friends. Not so. I was not then, nor am I now, a social animal. I didn't then, and I wouldn't now, know a "class act" if it jumped up and bit me on the nose, and Laura Benson was the quintessential, stereotypical nerd of the universe. She was a skinny, brilliant, humorless, spoiled, whining rich kid who needed an afternoon on the driveway with some red ants worse than anyone I ever knew. However, she had the books, and the good sense to know I couldn't stand her, and she left me alone to read. So, when Mother said, "Marti loves to visit Laura," you can probably picture the panic in my eyes when faced with a choice between Laura Benson or a hamburger and a Sunday drive with my father.

Some things in a relationship between a husband and wife can be settled with collective bargaining or knockdown, drag-out fighting; some things are "non-negotiables." My father's smoking and being with his friends were non-negotiables, his involvement in the union was a non-negotiable, his affection for me and subsequent tendency to refuse disciplining me was a non-negotiable. Visiting with some people from the church every so often was one of my mother's non-negotiables. The hamburger and the Sunday drive faded from my fantasy and I saw before me the endless afternoon with the Bensons *at our house,* so no librarial retreat. I would have to entertain Laura Benson. Jesus was getting back at me before we'd even discussed the little matter of my reluctant attendance at church; I didn't want to visit His house, so He'd bring the Bensons to mine. I think I'd rather have been knocked on my butt by a bolt of lightning.

We went to church. After services and Sunday School, Mother and Dad asked the Bensons to come over for lunch and a visit. They said yes and the afternoon was set; they would go home, change clothes, and be at our house shortly.

The things that happened that afternoon might never have happened if Bob hadn't called right after church to ask us to come over for a barbecue. My father knew better than to suggest calling the Bensons to cancel, so he didn't. But I think the combination of church, the Bensons, and missing a barbecue with his favorite people slightly unhinged him, and a terrible mischief entered his soul. He changed from my dear, hardworking, sensible father into Jack "Red" Reisz, Scourge of Lorain, Ohio, Terror of Steeltown, Mothers Everywhere Hide Your Daughters, Delight of His Brother's Life.

When the Bensons arrived, everything seemed fine. Dad even helped by bringing in the glasses of iced tea so that Mother could sit and visit. Everyone enjoyed the tea; they drank their first glass like there was no tomorrow. My mother had iced coffee instead. She never drank iced tea and was delighted when Lucy Benson said, "Mary, this tea is delicious! Where do you get it?"

"It *is* good, Little Mary," said Owen Benson. (He always called my mother "Little Mary" because he said she was "so dear that it just seemed a natural thing to call her." My father hated it when Owen Benson called her that. Probably because Mother liked it so much.)

Anyway, the Bensons loved the iced tea and asked Dad for seconds. Mother started to get up, but my father was going to be "of some help this time," he said, and went off to the kitchen to get refills. Down the hall, in my bedroom, Laura and I sat on the bed, staring at each other. She had changed from her yellow nylon church dress to a blue nylon "casual" dress. I had changed to jeans and couldn't figure out what we were going to do with each other for the next three or four hours. Suddenly, I heard loud, raucous laughing—real laughing. The Bensons never laughed, so I couldn't decide if we had company I hadn't seen yet, or what. I had to go investigate and, when I walked into the living room, I couldn't believe it! Owen Benson was sitting next to my mother on the couch; he had twisted his napkin into a moustache and was pretending to be the villain in one of those old time melodramas. My father was sitting next to Lucy Benson on the other couch telling her a story about the time he used to sell newspapers on the corner in front of the whorehouse and she was laughing—hard! Mother looked a little pleased and a little scared.

When I walked out, I must have looked a little confused myself because she said, "Marti, we're having such a good time. Mr. Benson is telling me about a play he was in in high school."

"Oh," I said.

"Could you get us some more iced tea, Honey?" Mother asked me. "Why don't you just bring the pitcher in here?"

"Sure," I said.

My father jumped up like he'd been shot. "I'll get it, Muggsy."

"She can help, Jack."

"I want to, Marsh. I always leave everything up to you. Let me do this little thing this time." And he was in the kitchen before she could say another word. My father was about as comfortable in the kitchen as a goldfish in a house full of cats and never, never, *never* entered it except for meals or a beer. The idea of him fixing iced teas was fascinating. I had to see him do it, so I followed him to the kitchen and poked my head around the corner. Dad was holding the pitcher of iced tea over the sink and pouring out a little of it. Then, he set it down and opened the cupboard where Mother kept the special china and the liquor. He took out a bottle and poured a cup or so into the iced tea and stirred it around a little. He turned around, pitcher in hand, and saw me standing there. "Muggsy!" he said. "Did you come in to help your old Dad? Here, Honey, carry this out to the Bensons."

"Why are you pouring that in it?" I asked. "Does Mother know?" "No, Muggsy. It's a surprise. We aren't going to tell Mother until later. Doesn't Mrs. Benson have a nice smile?"

"No," I said, and we went into the other room.

Mrs. Benson had loosened the top button of her blouse. She patted the couch next to her as Dad and I walked in. "Come here and sit down, Jack. What took you so long?" Mother gave her a look that would have frosted hot coals. Owen Benson had taken off his tie and untied his shoelaces. "Little Mary," he was saying, "we've got to get together more often." He patted her knee. Dad saw it and took out a cigarette. Mother smiled at me,

"Are you girls hungry? Lunch will be ready soon."

"Lunch!" squealed Mrs. Benson. "I couldn't eat a thing. Could you, Owen? Not a thing. I'll just finish up my tea and we'll be going. I feel a little sleepy and light-headed actually..." And she sneezed. When she sneezed, the strangest thing happened. It was as if the sneeze knocked her out. She sneezed, closed her eyes, put her head back on the couch and was immediately asleep.

"Oh my God!" said Mother. "Little Lucy!" said Owen and started laughing.

Mother got up. "I'll get some ice. I think she's fainted. Maybe it's the heat—she's probably hungry." Mother was beginning to panic. "Jack! Come here, please!" She called my father from the kitchen. "What could have happened? What do you think happened?" she asked him.

"I don't know, Hon." My father was trying hard not to laugh—Owen Benson was out in the living room laughing, to no one, at nothing in particular. "Jack, what would make her faint like that?"

"All that laughing, maybe." My father was about to say the wrong thing. "She probably busted something she hasn't used in a while—she never laughs."

"Jack," said my mother, "I don't know *what* you did, but I know you're responsible for this somehow. You didn't want them to come and you've done something. When I find out what it is—" She never finished the sentence. The laughing in the living room had stopped. My parents looked at each other in the silence.

Laura Benson walked quietly into our kitchen. "Mrs. Reisz," she said, "I think we should go home. Both my mother and my father have fallen asleep. Could you wake them, please?"

Mother looked at me, then at my father, then at Laura, then back at my father. She tried not to laugh. She tightened her lips, she cleared her throat, she coughed, she blinked hard.

My father grinned his most wicked grin. "I guess we must be real relaxing people to be around, Marsh." Mother picked up one of the iced tea glasses, sniffed it, tasted it, and put it down. "What do you say we wake up the Bensons, send them home, and call Bob to see if he still wants us. What do you say, Marsh?"

That's when she let go of it. Mother started laughing. "Oh, Jack," she choked and coughed and laughed some more, "you are the damndest, craziest, most immature man I have ever met in my life! What am I going to do with you?"

"I know it, Marcia, I know!" And they went out and roused the Bensons and sent them home. We only visited with them at *their* house after that and only once or twice. I guess once somebody falls asleep on your couch, you feel different about them or something.

Anyway, we went over to Bob's house then and ate hot dogs. When we got home, I went to bed and listened to my parents talk. "I'll never get over Lucy with her blouse unbuttoned," said my mother. "It's so unlike her."

"It's the best she's ever looked," said my father.

"I noticed you were certainly friendly with her all afternoon, Jack Reisz. Patting her hand and making goo-goo eyes at her. Her hair was all coming down, too—it looked silly."

"I don't know," said my father—he had this smile in his voice, "she reminded me a little bit of Ann Sheridan, the way she looked. Besides, you didn't seem to mind Owen Benson calling you 'Little Mary' all afternoon and putting his hand on your knee. Made himself pretty comfortable, loosening up his tie and his shoelaces like that."

"I've always thought Owen looked a lot like Cary

Grant." There was silence; I could hear Mother humming "They Wouldn't Believe Me," which was her favorite song. "He really is kind of cute for an older man," she said. And for a minute, right before I fell asleep, I could just see Mother putting on her little hat, the one with the veil that went over her eyes.

19

Domenic's— Six O'Clock

Dad worked 7:30 A.M. to 4:30 P.M. He showered right at the mill before he got home and sometimes he showered again at home to please Mother, who felt very strongly about cleanliness. On Thursday, which was payday, and on some Saturdays, Dad and the two zillion guys from the mill would get off work, shower, pick up their paychecks, cash them, and head for Domenic's. They could be there by 6:00 and, with luck, could be on the way to forgetting the foreman, the dirt, the too-small paycheck and the way it wouldn't cover the bills, by 6:45.

There used to be a song called "A Little Bit of Heaven." I was about eleven when it was popular and, every time I heard it, I saw Domenic's in my mind. It was a real small place, kind of dark inside, two gasoline pumps outside (the old, round kind—looked a little like shaving cream cans to me). I don't think they sold much gas—they didn't even have a "dinger" to tell when someone was out there. The customer would have to honk his car horn and, if Dom or his son heard it and felt like coming out from behind the bar, they'd sell some gas.

I don't know if Domenic's had always been a bar or not. They sold a lot of things, though. Behind the bar, shelves were crowded with all kinds of stuff: clocks with gold numbers, dolls with crocheted dresses, mugs and hand-painted dishes, watches—ladies' and men's—baseball caps, banks shaped like oranges, figurines with bare breasts and rhinestone G-strings, trays of rings and earrings, nylon stockings, gauzy scarves in bright colors, cigarettes, cigars (they were sold in silver tubes at 50 cents apiece), candy bars, gum, and Life Savers. Now, all of that was above and in back of the huge jars of hard-boiled eggs, dill pickles, big green olives, pink/grey pigs' feet, Polish sausages, packages of potato chips and peanuts, and wax-paper-wrapped bologna sandwiches. The bar itself was some kind of very dark wood: lots of varnish on it over a few carved names and telephone numbers. It was constantly being wiped and polished by Domenic or his son or his wife (well, *maybe* she was his wife. Dad said he thought they might be married, but with Domenic you just never knew).

Domenic seemed like a serious man to me. He had a big curved nose and little green eyes. His skin was so swarthy that his beard stubble looked green. He was short and square and looked tired a lot.

The woman in his life was named Carly. She was a first-degree floozy, blond variety, and could carry six beers at once from the bar to the table. My mother hated her with a passion she generally reserved for people like Hitler or the Vanderbilts or the neighbor lady. (My mother *always* hated the neighbor lady. I don't know exactly why. It had something to do, I believe, with an argument they once got into about the neighbor lady's cat, Grace, getting into our yard and sleeping on our chaise longue. I was a little bit allergic to cats and wasn't allowed to have one, and every time I'd lie down on the chaise longue I would sneeze and wheeze a little and my mother took it *very* personally that the neighbor lady wouldn't keep her cat at home even after mother explained the situation. I think that was the problem. Also, my father thought the neighbor lady was "hot stuff.")

Carly didn't pay a lot of attention to women other than a couple of her very close buddies. She'd walk up to the table, look at my dad, and say, "Whatcha havin', Jacky?" Dad would tell her, then she'd ask, "How 'bout her?" (meaning Mother). I mean, she wouldn't even look Mother's way. Dad would order and Carly would *reach across Mother* to tap me on the nose with the nine-inch scarlet fingernail of her right index finger, and say, "Whatcha want, Sweetie? It's on the house, whatever it is. God, Jacky! How'd an ugly guy like you get such a cute little girl?" Then she'd take my order and walk off to get it all with never a word or a look that acknowledged Mother's presence. My mother used to say the reason for that was that Carly was intimidated by a truly decent woman. Dad used to say he didn't think that was it.

I never saw anyone slide a beer on the bar in Domenic's, but I'll bet you could have done it. It was a pretty long bar, maybe twenty-five stools—the spinning kind, green leather tops—and was the best place to sit because you could talk to Domenic if you sat there. Otherwise, you couldn't because he never came out from behind the bar —*never*. [I once asked my dad, what does he do when he has to go to the bathroom? Bob Butler said, "Honey, he just pisses in a bucket behind the bar." Then I asked, "Who has to empty it?" and Bob said, "It doesn't have to be emptied, Sweetheart. He serves it to the customers." My Uncle Gib almost died laughing when he said that so I knew it had to be a joke. But Mother almost wiped out everyone with the Look.]

So, it was better to sit at the bar. If it was too crowded, there were six or eight booths along the walls. People would move over to them if they got to talking and were going to go to somebody's house later or were going to make a party someplace else. Or, it was better to sit in the booths if you had your kid and wife with you, which my father sometimes did. There was probably a law about juveniles in bars, but Domenic didn't seem to care much about it because he never said anything about my being there. He was a funny guy anyway. He was a short man—Greek, Dad said. But Andy told us, "He ain't no Greek, he's a Mexican. Don't let him kid you."

Dad said, "Bullshit, Andy. The man *speaks* Greek, for God's sake. You just hate Greeks since that little Greek asshole hit you with that piece of pipe."

"Damn near killed me," said Andy. "Chased me a mile and a half down the street and all I did was try to take out his damn daughter."

"Goddam it, Andy, that was his wife and you knew it! You got balls for brains."

We laughed so hard. I don't know how to put on paper how hard we laughed—even Mother. The vision of Andy running for his life with some guy shouting at him in Greek and waving a piece of pipe was ridiculous. Andy showed us the scar on the back of his head. "Twelve stitches! Jesus, what I do for women!"

Mother laughed so hard she had to go to the bathroom. She laughed all evening and on the way home in the car, too. We even got to stop for spaghetti—she was laughing that much.

My mother laughing was a reason I loved Domenic's.

20

I've Never Seen the Statue of Liberty

In 1961, I graduated from high school. I went to a junior college for a year and then decided to go away to school. I chose a college in Northern California, announced my decision to my parents, and made plans. Almost everyone leaves home, right? I mean, everyone decides at some time in their lives that they need to experience the world in their own way, on their own terms, and not on the terms of their parents. So, they go away to school, or off to an exciting career somewhere, or they join the navy, or get married. I was no different.

Psychologists say that, in order for it to be possible for a child to leave home, he or she has to hate it a little. They say that no one would ever leave home if it just kept on feeling good to be there, so it has to start *not* feeling good. I think that must be a new thing. I'm pretty old— over 40—and a lot of things didn't happen to me that are supposed to be the things that happen to everybody, like hating my parents so that I could leave home, or jumping into new and bizarre religions as a protest against the way I was brought up. Anyway, I didn't come to hate my folks and everything they stood for or think that we just didn't relate to each other, or anything like that. I just figured I couldn't live with them forever—I didn't know any adults who lived with their parents except for my girlfriend's oldest sister, who kept marrying people and leaving them, so she moved in and out of her parents' house on a sort of regular basis—so I needed to learn to be what I wanted to be and then get out on my own.

I don't know if I'd have been certain on my own that it was time to strike out for independence, but things around me began to change and those changes probably gave me a nudge or two.

My father's friends quieted down and, with them, union activities. It had been years since we'd gone through a strike or worried about Dad walking a picket line. The union negotiated and management cooperated, which was a lot easier on my father and his buddies, but much less exciting for me.

Dad stopped occasionally for a beer after work at a new place—not Domenic's—closer to home. Bob had got married and so had Billy Marshall, and their wives were "nice women" who didn't like the idea of their husbands spending time at a beer joint, so they didn't hang out at Domenic's anymore. The guys who did were all new guys whom my father didn't know very well. Bob even had kids; I don't know if Billy did or not, but Bob did and, when they came over, there was lots less colorful language and a softening of the tales that were told. Bob stopped threatening to break my arm and I was cautioned before each visit *not* to mention the women friends he'd brought over in the past.

Andy didn't get married, but he began keeping company with the same woman on a regular basis. Her name was Rosemarie and her favorite color was pink. My father said that she'd catch Andy and make him marry her one day. I didn't think so. Andy and Rosemarie came to visit on holidays and special occasions, but they left early.

Everyone seemed to leave a little earlier than they used to and I didn't lay in bed anymore and listen to uproarious laughter and funny old union songs with slightly dirty lyrics.

My dashing, debonair Uncle Gib still drove a yellow Buick convertible, but he said he couldn't drink like he used to and had to be careful to stay sober for the drive home. He and my aunt came to visit less and less because his health wasn't good. He spent a lot of time on the weekends resting or going for long rides up the coast. We didn't see them nearly as often as I wanted to.

Before I left home, Mother gave a party for me. After the party got started and everyone was having a good time, my uncle said to me, "Let's take a ride to the liquor store, kiddo." We got into his car with the white real-leather upholstery and took off. After a minute or two of driving in silence, he said, "It's not the kind of party we used to have in the old days, is it, Honey?" I said no. "Well," he said, "things change. I guess it's time for you to go off and find your own parties. Believe me, kiddo, they're out there. You go out and find them."

When we stopped the car at the liquor store, I put my arms around his neck and hugged him. "I love you," I said. "I really love you and Aunt Marie better than almost anyone in the world."

"Well, you'll get smarter when you get older, I guess. You'll pick who you love a little more carefully. Let's see if they've got anything good here." And we got out of the car to go into the store.

"Uncle Gibby," I asked, "what kind of shave lotion do you wear? You always smell good."

He laughed. "It's something special. It's double martinis—straight up."

A few years later, on my wedding, I was to ask him the same question. I got the same answer then and have since put it into a poem about him—a poem about a hero.

IN THE LONG HOUSES OF THE SHOSHONE

Consider the following:
A sail across the San Fernando Valley

151

in November to Uncle Gib's funeral
since he let himself die of cigarette smoke
and yellow Buick convertibles. His eyes
might be closed very tight;
maybe pastries and cold cuts after and time for all
to eat. What an idler I am!
This funeral is a nearwelcome break;
I was going to vacuum and spray for roaches
today. He will be lying flat, rosary
in his fine long fingers. My beautiful
womanizing uncle of the delicately drawn mustache.

You would hate Morro Bay except for the golf
course, knowing that the fishing boats there are making
those warm moaning noises. You would hate it,
think it drab and lacking excitement.
What an intrusion this death of yours!
I protest it. I will make a fine speech in despair.
Walking with you to the liquor
store, I never could take your hand—(handsome
some hand. Why does that mean good-looking?) My
hands: quick-bitten nails, have always done a disappearing
act around you. This highway is a river.
It does not stop. Maybe I will follow it
clear to a real river and skip your party
altogether. We can be no Pietà.

Though once, when I married, you held me. I said
what cologne is it you always wear: You said
Honey, that cologne is called double martinis
straight up. (To tell the truth I am a little
drunk more than a little I guess.) I do not
know if you like poetry; I wish I were
published and famous and could bring a book
of my work signed to you. See how we sail together
denying each other? November is so much
rot—month of denial or approbation.
I may never mention your name again.
I may sit at the fireplace, your grey suits
will be on my mind and I will listen to

Hindemith or Mahler, my house shaking—tumbling
around me all the things in it becoming
polished and gem-like that way becoming bits
and debris.
The pinyon-juniper forests on Shoshone land
have been destroyed. I read that. I promised
at home to do this alone. No more your name
be uncle to me.

Now, then: leaving home. I had decided to be a teacher—maybe high school English—and was going to live in a dorm. I would leave one week before the fall semester began so I could get into my room and get settled. My Uncle Phillip and Aunt Jan would drive me up there on their way to a vacation, so I'd be saying good-bye to my parents at home. I think they planned it that way so we wouldn't have to say good-bye at the door of a car in front of a dormitory. I started cleaning my room and packing what I'd absolutely have to have for the next few years, and while doing that, I came across my diaries. I hadn't kept one in several years, but the old ones had been faithfully kept from the time I was about seven years old until I reached thirteen or fourteen, when I decided that only "children" kept diaries. There were long, rambling descriptions of parties and people and stories and jokes and songs. There were brief notes to remind myself to "be nicer to Mom and help her around the house," and notes that were full of cryptic initials: "I hate R.G. He's mean and took the quarter that dropped out of my stupid pocket during lunch. I thought I liked him, but S.L. can have him now." There was a page with only these words on it: "PAULETTE STINKS!" And there was this: "Bob told a joke to Daddy about a lady who fell in love with a sailor who only had one leg. That was the only part that was funny." And: "Dad will be home now. We are on strike. Mom cried. We had cottage cheese and noodles for dinner." And: "Dad told Billy that I was crying because Brian B. said I had a nose like an anteater. Billy said I have the most beautiful nose in the world. He said that in the future, men will come from all over the world and fall in love with me for my nose and that they will put Brian B. in jail for saying bad things about it. Billy Marshall is nuts, but I started laughing anyway."

There was page after page of that kind of stuff. I read through all of them. Finally, I put them in a paper sack and took them out to the trash and continued to clean and pack. The next day, my father came to my room with the paper sack full of diaries. "Tell you what, Muggsy," he said, "I'll just hang on to these and I bet you a quarter you'll ask me for them some day."

"No, I won't, Dad. They're so dumb."

"Let's make a bet."

"OK. We have a bet."

"Remind me, before you go, to tell you a real funny story about a bet I made once. Me and that crazy Lou... he bet me that I couldn't get to first base with a girl named Cora who was half Puerto Rican, half Scandahoovian, Catholic, and meaner than the meanest sonofabitch I ever met." Dad sat down on the bed. "This gal was about five foot nine and she had black hair and real black eyes. When her folks got together, they made one pretty girl between them. She was a real beauty. But, I don't know, she was some kind of man-hater or something. Lou always said she was probably a dyke—you know what that is, Honey? [Yes, Daddy, I'm eighteen years old forheavenssake.] But I always thought she just hadn't found the right man. So, me and Lou used to go to this place where she worked, sort of a little café and bar kind of place, and we'd watch her wait on people and we'd try to talk to her. Hell! She wouldn't even give us a little polite conversation. Finally, I said to Lou 'What'll you give me if I can get Cora to go out with me?' He said, 'Jack, you won't even be able to get her to talk to you.' I said, 'Yes I will. Wanna bet?' 'You're on,' he says, 'I'll bet you a buck you can't take her out.' I said, 'It's a bet.'

"The next night we go into this place, and there she was like always. I walked up to her and said, 'Look, I'm a pretty nice guy. Most people like me and I have never done any real harm on purpose to anybody. I've lived

154

around here all my life and made a lot of friends. All I want to do is take you to a movie or somethin'. I'm not going to bite you or anything. Could we maybe just go to a movie or somethin'?'

She looked at me real funny. Then she said, 'You been comin' in here a lot. You come in to see me?' I said yes. She said, 'OK. We'll go out, but no funny business.' I turned around and I gave Lou this big wink to let him know that I won the bet. He started laughing and I turned around to tell Cora when I'd pick her up and stuff. I turned around and—Jesus Christ!—this girl hits me right in the mouth and she's wearin' knuckles—*brass* knuckles, like in the movies. I went down on the floor and she started hollering her head off—'You sonsofbitches! You bastards! Make a bet on me, willya! Well, I'll show you who to bet on!' Hell! If I hadn't stayed on the floor and covered up my head with my jacket, she'd probably have killed me.

"Old Lou came running over—'You all right, Jacky? She sure cut your mouth up. You OK? She must have heard us betting. I don't know how she heard...' Well, by that time I was on my feet and checking out if my teeth were all there, which they were, and trying to figure out how the hell she heard us. My shirt was a mess—Ma just about killed me—and we left the place. When we got out to the car, Louie said, 'I guess you owe me a buck, but I'll forget it because she almost knocked your head off and I didn't think that would happen.' I said 'Me too,' and that was the end of it.

"I don't know why I remembered that story just now except that we made that bet about your, uh, whatchamacallits there."

"*Diaries*, Dad."

"Yeah, diaries. You wrote all that stuff down, huh? I mean about Andy and the mill and Uncle Gib and your mama and me. All that stuff you heard us talk about, you wrote it down?"

"A lot of it, yeah."

"I'll be damned. I never knew you did that. Well, I'll

just hang on to them. You might want them sometime. Who knows?"

Before I left home, my mother wanted to throw a party for me. She wanted to ask a whole lot of people and do it up right with Polish food and all my friends. She told me to make up a guest list of everyone I wanted there and they would be invited—no matter how many people it was. Then she said I should make up a list of the foods I wanted and she'd cook all of it and my aunt would help. So I made up a guest list of all the people I wanted at my farewell party and a list of all the foods I wanted to eat. It read like this:

Guests	Food
Andy Kushner and friend	*Kielbasa—baked*
Bob Butler and wife	*Pork and Beans*
Billy Marshall and wife	*City Chicken*
Uncle Gib and Aunt Marie	*Stuffed Cabbage Rolls*
Uncle Phillip and Aunt Jan	*Potato Pancakes*
David (my boyfriend)	*Bologna Sandwiches*
Dory (my best girlfriend)	*Cottage Cheese and Noodles*
Karen (my other best girlfriend)	*Potato Chips*
Soupy Sales	

I gave the list to Mother and we sat down at the kitchen table to talk it over. She started to cry.

"What's wrong?" I said. "What did I do?"

"These are mostly *our* friends, Honey. You don't have to ask them. Ask *your* friends."

"Oh," I said.

"And this food. Marti, it's all the cheap stuff that I had to cook for us all those years when Daddy wasn't earning much or he'd be on strike. You don't have to ask for this stuff now."

"Chips are expensive," I said. "The potato chips are expensive. You hate to buy them because they cost so much."

She cried harder. "We can have a ham or steaks,

156

Honey, or a big roast beef. I can make pierogi, we can have anything you'd like."

"I *like* cottage cheese and noodles. I like bologna on bread with mustard. I like City Chicken—I didn't used to think I did, but I do. Don't cry, Mom."

She cried anyway. "And this guest list... We took up your whole life with *our* friends and didn't give you a chance to make friends of your own. How could we be so selfish. I feel terrible."

"Mom," I said, "please, please stop crying. I thought they were *my* friends, too. I don't want a party if we can't have those people. Please, Mom, stop crying."

She didn't. "Who's Soupy Sales?" she said. "Have we met him?"

21

The Last of
the East Side Kids

The thing to remember here is that the party was for me, who was leaving home to go to college. I was leaving people I didn't want to leave for reasons I wasn't sure of. I felt like I was taking medicine instead of starting a wonderful new adventure and, while I knew it was probably the right thing to do, it was hard to keep in mind why I was doing it at all.

The party was planned for a Saturday afternoon in July. Bob's wife worked in a bakery so she was bringing a huge cake. Mother had done all the cooking, with some help from my Aunt Jan; Uncle Gib and Aunt Marie were bringing wine and booze and beer. My father had brought my record player outside on the patio and polka dancing music was playing.

I walked all around the backyard, talking to everybody, drinking a beer—just like the big folks, just like I always wanted to be the other thousand times all those people were at our house celebrating all the things they celebrated—and I got sad. I didn't want the beer, or the grown-up tight skirt I was wearing, or the plans for my future; I didn't want a boyfriend and my own place and my own bank account and me telling myself what to do, with nobody to interfere.

I looked over at Uncle Gib telling a joke to Andy. He was bending toward him with a wonderful wiseass smile and Andy was all ready to start laughing before he even heard the punch line. Little Billy Marshall had a bottle of beer in his hand and his arm around his tall, skinny wife, Shirley, who had at least four inches on Little Billy and who laughed at everything anybody said, whether it was funny or not. Bob was leaning his elbow on my friend Karen and telling her the story about the time he and my father used three lunch hours to fill out the subscription cards in all the magazines they could find and have those magazines sent to the foreman's house. He was telling the story as quietly as he possibly could because my Uncle Phil, who was management, knew that particular foreman pretty well. My father was talking to my Uncle Joe and Aunt Marge, who didn't come to see us very often. They lived in Culver City and had stood up with my parents on their wedding day. My Uncle Joe was the teeniest little guy I ever saw—skinny and bald with a temper like a mongoose. My Aunt Marge was a soft, pink, round lady who smiled a lot and had a wide space between her front teeth which I thought made her look English (from England) and therefore sophisticated. My friend Dory was talking to my boyfriend over in the corner of the yard. She was wearing black—she always wore black because she thought it made her look thin. I thought it made her look overheated. Dory was one of the smartest girls I'd ever known. She got straight A's in school and had read everything James Joyce ever wrote. She wrote poetry and drank bourbon and liked men. She told me once that she would never go to bed with a man who hadn't read T.S. Eliot's *The Waste Land* in at least one other language besides English. I asked her if she *knew* any men who could speak any other language besides English. She told me that that wasn't exactly the point. All of our conversations were sort of like that. She was talking to my boyfriend, David, about considering suicide as an alternative to college because life was so meaningless and all; he was listening politely and nodding his head. "Camus says...you know Camus?" she asked. "No," said David. "Doesn't matter. Camus says there is only one decision any individual ever has to make and that is whether or not to commit suicide." "Or maybe whether or not to have another beer," said David. They laughed. My mother and my Aunt Jan were in the kitchen arguing loudly about what kind of bowl the potato salad should go in.

I went over to the place where I used to squat down and hide so I could hear and see everything that was going on. It was the same scene I'd watched a hundred times—the same people. My father had just mowed the back lawn and hosed down the patio to keep the flies away. Mother had put cheesecloth over the food, and they'd put the beer and the bottles of pop in a big stainless steel tub next to the food table. There was so much laughter; it seemed to ride on the air like a colored kite, floating up and over the clouds, never really stopping, just hesitating in one or two spots and then taking off again into the sky. I wanted everybody to stay right where they were forever—right there in the backyard so that I could get up every morning and look at them and listen to them and know that nothing *good* ever really had to change.

"What's up, Muggsy?" It was my father. "You stick that lip out any further, a pigeon's gonna come roost on it."

I laughed. A little.

"What's wrong, Honey? You don't like the party?"

"It's a wonderful party."

"Maybe you like it too much, huh? Maybe it'd just be nice for this party to go on forever and you wouldn't go anyplace and none of us would get old or change or nothing. That it?"

I nodded yes.

"I always told myself I was going to take you to New York City to see the Statue of Liberty. I never did it. I

160

never could make enough money for a trip like that. You gotta see it sometime, Muggs. It's really something."

"OK, Dad," I said.

"Did I ever tell you the story about the time your Aunt Marie went to Cleveland to get a job and be on her own?"

"No."

"Well, I'll tell you what happened. About the time your Aunt Marie turned twenty-one, she had just finished going to a secretarial school. She'd learned typing and shorthand and all that kind of stuff and she was working in Lorain for an insurance office. The office was owned by a guy who just couldn't seem to make his hands behave, if you get my meaning, Muggsy. He kept pestering your Aunt Marie, who'd come home from work and tell our oldest sister about it. The guy was going to fire her if she didn't cooperate and be a little friendlier to him, he was going to tell everyone in town that she was cheap, he was going to do this, that, and the other thing. Marie was frantic. Jobs weren't easy to come by then and she didn't know what she'd do if he spread her name all over town. Finally, my sis, Elizabeth, said to her, 'Marie, that's how it is living in a small town. Everybody's everybody else's friend. You smear somebody's reputation and it's all over the place before you know it. Maybe you ought to think about moving to a bigger place where you could get a better job.' So, Marie thought about it.

"She decided that Elizabeth was right and that she'd move to a big city where *nobody'd* know who she was. She figured she could get a real good job and her own place."

"Nobody's smearing my name all over town, Dad."

"Don't be impatient. This is a good story. You always want to know the end too fast. Anyway, so she went to Cleveland one weekend, found herself a job and a room, and came home to pack her stuff. Hell, it only took her a day to get everything together. I went upstairs to start bringing her suitcases and junk down and she was sitting on the damn bed crying her eyes out."

"I haven't cried once, Dad," I said.

"You might be, Muggsy, if you keep on interrupting

my story. Anyway, I said to her, 'What the hell are you crying about? Bill and Elizabeth are going to be here any minute to pick you up.' She said, 'What if I don't want to go, Jacky? What if I want to stay right here with you and Louie and Mama and Daddy?' 'So?' I said to her, 'So what?' 'Jacky! Everybody'll think I'm a baby,' she said. 'Mama's going to think I'll be here forever, sponging off her and Daddy. Elizabeth is going to think...' Well, sure as hell, my dad heard her. He could hear crying a mile away if it was one of us kids. He came up the stairs and into Marie's room. He asked her in Hungarian what was wrong. She told him in Hungarian, crying the whole damn time. He was quiet for a minute, then he came over and sat down next to her. He put his arm around her and started to talk to her real quiet. Then, he patted her hair and they both laughed. She went downstairs and told Bill that, thank you very much, she wasn't going to Cleveland after all. She didn't leave home for a couple more years."

"So?"

"So what?"

"Daddy, what did Grandpa say to her? How come she didn't go?"

"Oh, that. He said to her 'Marie, my darling, young birds are pushed out of their nests when it comes time for them to go; hyenas abandon their young so they'll leave and start their own lives; weasels leave their young out in the wilderness to make their own way. Your mama and I love you. We are not birds or hyenas or weasels, and you may stay here as long as you live, if it's what you want.' And you know what, Muggsy?"

"What?"

"Your mama and I aren't birds or hyenas or weasels, either. OK?"

"OK, Dad," I said. He got up and started to go back to the party.

"Daddy?" I said.

"What?"

"I liked the story."

"Me too, Muggsy. Except you always want to know the end too fast."

Dad and I went back to the party after that. It got dark and the food was all gone and the beer was all gone and everybody had to be going home. I said "Good-bye" and "I'll write" to everybody there and it was all over as simply as that.

I left at nine the next morning. My aunt and uncle pulled up in the driveway in their big green station wagon and put my suitcases and boxes in it and it was time to go. I was not much of a crier then. I am more so now. But then, I figured, if I started, my mother would start and she took a long time to finish once she got started and I didn't want to leave my father with that, so I tried not to cry.

"Bye, Mom," I said.

"It was a very nice party, wasn't it, Honey?"

"It was the best one we ever had, Mom. Honest."

"Are you wearing clean underwear?"

"Mother!"

"Well, you know...I don't want to get a call from some hospital somewhere this afternoon and have to go down to identify you in some morgue somewhere and see you have on dirty underwear."

"Mom, I'm wearing clean underwear."

"Well, take care of yourself. Eat and sleep and take those vitamins."

"I will, Mom." She started crying. Hard.

"I love you, you know. You're the best daughter in the world and I love you."

"Don't cry, Mom," I said. "I know. I love you, too. OK? Don't cry." Then I hugged my father. "Bye, Daddy," I said. "I'm sure going to miss you."

"Bye, Muggsy," he said. "Me too. Nobody laughs at my jokes like you do. Listen now, you remember—you always laugh first, Honey. Nobody can laugh at you if you're laughing first. When you meet people, you meet 'em laughing."

Then I was crying. "You're crazy," I said, "but I love you."

"I know it." He smiled. "Hey, something else, too. You be proud of where you come from. Don't you ever forget your Daddy was one of the first fifty guys ever hired at Kaiser Steel in Fontana and a dues-paying, active member of the United Steelworkers of America. Don't you forget that."

"I won't, Daddy. I won't ever forget that. I'll see you guys at Thanksgiving."

And that was that. I hugged them both again and got in the car.

The last thing Mother said was, "Did that Soupy Sales person ever come? Did we meet him?"

I hung out the window and waved until we turned the corner. Then I sang of lavender this and lavender that and of kings and queens all the way to San Jose.

22

Kate Smith—
An Afterword

My father is eighty-one years old. He looks sixty. We were sitting on the sofa in my parents' living room when I showed him these stories. "Muggsy," he said, "I hope to God nobody comes looking for me after they read this. You've got stuff in here I never even thought you heard. How'd you remember all that stuff?" I told him it was easy to remember because it was so much fun. I told him that those were the happiest days of my whole life and that sometimes I laughed just thinking about them. He laughed. You ought to hear my father laugh; it's a laugh he brings out of some Open Hearth somewhere. Everybody starts laughing when he does. "I was always worried you were going to look back on all of that like it was a real black time. We were so goddam broke all the time. Seemed like we never went anywhere...never could buy you anything. I don't know" —he thought for a little while, smoking and smiling and shaking his head—"I don't know...Anyway, you wrote those things real good, real fine. Old Andy would've liked them and so would Bob. All the guys—great guys... You know, some of those, uh, 'floozies'"—he laughs again—"those gals... well, Bob finally married his girlfriend and so did Little Billy. That damn Andy never did. Can you believe it, he never did. He was at least sixty-five, maybe seventy years old, and he was still messing around with some of those old broads."

My mother's voice: "Jack..."

"Some of them looked pretty good for their age, too. That one gal... what was her name—Lafathe, Rosemarie Lafathe. Andy took her out for—Jesus!—ten years anyhow. Never would marry her, either. She'd get all tanked up and pissed off at him and tell him she was never going to see him again and then go out with him three hours later. I never did figure out what that ugly old sonofabitch had that women liked. Mother never did like him, did you, Marsh? She never trusted Andy. You know, I always thought Andy was kind of sweet on your mother."

"Jack! You stop it!"

My father was laughing again. "Really, no really! I think he was real sweet on your mother. Well, she looked so good—like a movie star. She always had so much class, held herself so tall and was so careful with her clothes and all. I think Andy liked her." Dad lit up another cig. "You remember Kate Smith, Honey? That woman could sing. That was *real* singing. Not like this noise you hear all the time now. No sir, she could sing. She almost came out to the union hall once to sing. Remember, Marsh? BIG WOMAN. Big nationwide strike was on then... all across the country. *Everybody* was out of work—it was a real nasty one, too. There was a lot of fighting and rock throwing and going to jail. A lot of people lost their homes during that one; we were real lucky, your mom borrowed enough money to get us through so we didn't lose anything except a lot of sleep. Mom there, she charmed Pete the butcher into loaning us enough to make house payments."

"That's enough, Jack," said my mother.

"Well, you did. We shopped there all the time, of

course. Even when we weren't on strike, we shopped at Martinez's. Your mom insisted on it, Muggsy. So, when we were out of money, they carried us—let us charge it. But your mother was something. Old Pete never did see anything as good-looking as your mother. His Sally was about four foot tall and weighed three hundred pounds easy. So, when Mother'd walk in there with her hair all done up and those high heels, why old Pete would just about drop his meat cleaver and trip over his own feet to get over there and wait on her. 'How 'bout some nice filet today, Mrs. Reisz? We got some beautiful veal today, too—I cut it real thin just like you like it. How 'bout it, Mrs. Reisz? What you like today?' Your mom would smile and bat her eyes a little bit and say 'Well, thank you, Pete. I think that veal *does* sound nice. Remember, real thin, now.' Hell! Half the time, I don't think he rang the stuff up. I teased Mom so much over that guy, she almost killed me a couple times. Poor Mother! I gave her such a bad time over most everything. I'm over eighty, but I think I still can give her a bad time. [He can and does.]

"Anyway, that was a bad strike that time—lasted so damn long and surplus food supplies for the families were getting low and the guys were all pretty short-tempered. The union rep came to a meeting one night and was lucky to get out of there with his skin. Everybody was yelling at him and calling him names and it looked like it could get bad. He was trying to talk about how they were doing so good in the talks and how it should all be resolved very soon and how all we had to do was stick together. Nobody seemed to be buying that—they kept getting madder. Me and Andy and a big Mexican guy, Jesus, went to stand at the back of the hall in case there was any trouble."

"You were hoping, Dad, and you know it . . ."

"Some of the men had started stamping their feet and yelling *'No more talk! No more talk!'* Finally, when it looked like things were going to get bad, the guy says, 'Wait a minute, wait a minute. I got a surprise for you guys. The next union meeting is going to be for the families. We're gonna have food and beer and punch for the kids!' The guys started booing him. 'Wait a minute—there's something else, too. We're gonna have a special guest star to come entertain you people.' It got a lot quieter then. Somebody yelled *You gonna pay 'em with union dues, Buddy?'*

"'We don't have to pay nobody. They're gonna do it for free.'

"Somebody else yelled, *'Who you got for us, Mickey Mouse?'*

"'Naw, naw.' You could see the rep sweating over this one. 'We got somebody you're all gonna love. Your union knows what you guys like and we got somebody real good for you.' The place was pretty quieted down by this time and I was waiting to see who he was going to come up with. I thought he'd really cooked his own goose. How the hell is he going to get out of this?

"*'Who the hell is it, then?'* somebody hollered.

"'Well, I was leavin' it for a surprise but you dumbos ruined it already,' he says. 'Here goes. It's…it's…*KATE SMITH!'*"

My father was laughing again—Mother and I were laughing, too. It was just like the old days: Dad telling some crazy story and us being shocked and delighted and entertained for hours. "Oh no!" I said. "Not Kate Smith, Dad. How could he have said that? Oh no!"

"Those union reps would say *anything*," said Mother. "I mean *anything*. They didn't much care how believable it was."

"Well," said Dad, "everybody was real happy then. They called the meeting to a close and then started leaving. We were all saying how the union always comes through and how they really did care about us and our families—stuff like that. We were all talking about how Kate Smith must be a pretty good old gal to come all the way out to Fontana for a union meeting and how nobody was going to want to miss that. Well, my God, Muggsy, we'd all seen Kate Smith on television—everybody watched her. She wasn't just a singer, she was part of everybody's family. I think we all felt sort of related to her or something. Anyway, we went home and told our wives and our kids about it and we planned to all meet at somebody's house for potluck before the meeting. I mean, it was going to be a real occasion. The women were all talking about what to wear and how to do their hair. We were all thinking what we were going to say to Kate if we got to talk to her. Everybody was telling their kids how to behave while Kate was singing and how to shake hands if they got a chance to meet her. For the whole month, we just about forgot that we weren't working or eating very well or paying our bills. We were going to see Kate Smith!"

"Dad, am I going to like the end of this?"

"You've been asking me that for forty years, Honey. It doesn't seem to matter what I answer, you always want to hear the end anyway. Listen to this—it's finally the night she's supposed to come sing. The parking lot is jammed full up with cars. Everybody is there. All the families with the kids and everybody is all excited. We'd all had a few drinks at home to get ready for the big evening. Hell! Even your mother, there, she'd had a drink or two to celebrate. When we got up toward the doors of the hall, I could see the people standing around and looking mad. They're saying things like, *What the hell is this! I knew it! Goddam union screwed us again!*' I told your mom to hang on to you and I walked up to the doors. There was a big sign on the door that said KATE SMITH WILL NOT AP-PEAR TONIGHT. SHE GOT TONSILLITIS AND CANCELED THE SHOW. MEET AT THE FONTANA BOWL BOWLING ALLEY FOR FREE BOWLING TO ALL UNION MEMBERS AND THEIR FAMI-LIES. Godalmighty, I thought there was going to be a riot. I hoped that damned rep wouldn't have the balls to show up anywhere in the next year because someone would kill him for sure. You should've seen it—kids were crying, the ladies were crying, your mother was crying—Shit! Some of the guys looked like they were going to cry!

"Well then, the next thing we know, some guy is standing up by the door—I can't recall his name...little guy...a custodian out at the plant, I think—he stood there for a minute and then he said, 'I don't know about you guys, but I promised my wife and kids an evening out of the house and they're damn well gonna get it even if it is at goddam Fontana Bowl. We been waitin' a month for something good to happen and it ain't gonna be a goddam fist fight in the parking lot of the goddam union hall if I can help it. Now let's go bowling!'

"That's about all it took. I don't think any of us could stand our families being more disappointed than they already were. Hell, if we'd just gone home, we would have just sat there and felt lousy, so almost everybody headed for the bowling alley. The lanes were all open, the beer was a dime for union members and families, so we all sat around grousing and griping and drinking and bowling.

"We all felt pretty sad and we were all pretty quiet until the union rep walked in. All hell broke loose. There was the dirtiest cussing I ever heard and threats and guys getting ready to throw their beers at him. It didn't look good. People were yelling ugly stuff about the union and saying *She never was coming, was she, you asshole? Kate Smith was never even supposed to come at all, was she?'*

"The union rep didn't even look scared. He just stood there. He finally said, 'Whyn't you all shut up! You got wives and kids here. Why ain't you watchin' your goddam mouths! Shut up! All of ya', shut up!'

"The mood the guys were in, he shouldn't have been telling them to shut up. He should have been running in the other direction, but, the guy had balls, I have to give him that. [At seventy-three, my mother can still level a three-story building with the Look; my father was getting it as the story progressed.]

"'Now listen!' the rep started to say, 'Kate Smith was too supposed to come. Kate Smith loves the union. Her old man was a union man and she was going to do us a show for free, but she got this, uh, whatchamacallit... tonsillitis, and couldn't sing nothin', but she figured you bein' union people and all, well...she figured you'd understand. *She's* the one suggested bowling for Chrissakes and you guys are all bitchin' and pissin' around about it. *She's* the one said that union guys love bowling and if we treated you all to a few beers and a few lanes you'd be real pleased. She even said I should have you all sing "God Bless America" after you was done bowling in honor of her not bein' here an' all. Well, she ain't gonna under-

stand it when we tell her that you *wasn't* real pleased—
that you looked a gift horse in the mouth so to speak. No
sir. Old Kate's not gonna understand it at all.'

"Muggsy," said my father, "I didn't know if those
guys were going to kill him or cry or what. I looked over
at Little Billy Marshall and Bob and Andy and I saw they
were all laughing. Bob was mopping his eyes, he was
laughing so hard. I asked Andy what the hell was so
funny and he said, 'That crazy rep. He must think we got
about as much brains as these bowling balls to buy that
story. "God Bless America"! Oh my God, Jacky, I'm gonna
die laughing!'

"Well, I started laughing then and so did Mother and
so did everybody else. The rep just stood there, trying to
look like—I don't know—smart or something. The whole
place was laughing. Jesus, did we ever laugh!

"Then the rep says, 'I got somethin' else to say, so
shut up!'

"It quieted down a little. Somebody yelled, *What
would you like us to sing for Kate, you dumb bastard?'* and
everybody laughed again. [I'm sure it was my father who
yelled that.]

"'OK, OK. That's enough! I got somethin' to tell you
people. Strike's over—they signed the contract at seven
tonight while you was all bitchin' and carryin' on because
you didn't get to see Kate Smith. Now whaddaya think of
your union, you bastards!'

"Boy! Everyone went crazy! There was hooting and
hollering and laughing and crying and all kinds of noise-
making. All the ladies and kids were bawling their heads
off and the guys were pouring beer all over each other
and rolling the bowling balls everyplace but down the
lanes. Some of the guys had run up to the rep and were
buying him beers and slapping him on the back. Andy
and Bob were singing "God Bless America" at the top of
their lungs! It was a real circus. I'll never forget that if I
live to be a hundred." My father shook his head. "I was so
happy to have that strike over and done with. I think it
was the longest one we ever went through, wasn't it,
Hon?"

"But, Dad, what about Kate Smith? Did the union really arrange to have her there or not? Was she really going to come sing and did she really get tonsillitis? Was her father really a union man and all that?"

"Oh yeah, Kate Smith... Well, I'll tell you, Honey, I don't know. I never did really know."

"What! After all of that... Dad! What do you *think*? At least tell me that."

"I think, well... maybe... I'm not... I think we had more goddam Kate Smith records at the union hall dances after that than we had anything else and I think, if that crazy Bob had sung 'God Bless America' one more time, I'd have broken all those damned records over his head." He smiled a huge smile. "I was so glad to have that strike over with that I threw a party your mother will never forget. Remember that one, Marsh? The one where Gib and Bob put on the dresses and went over to St. George's Church for Saturday night Mass and the priest asked Gib if he was new to the parish and Gib told him he was your long-lost faggot brother and gave him our phone number? I think the guy's name was Father Dorset or something like that and he called you, remember that? Christ, Marsh! I thought you were going to..."

My father began another story.